OAK

Reaktion's Botanical series is the first of its kind, integrating
horticultural and botanical writing with a broader account
of the cultural and social impact of trees, plants and flowers.
Accessibly written yet encompassing the latest scholarship,
each title features around 100 fine images.

Published

Oak Peter Young
Geranium Kasia Boddy

Forthcoming

*Lily, Yew, Pine, Willow, Palm,
Orchid* and others

OAK

Peter Young

REAKTION BOOKS

Published by
REAKTION BOOKS LTD
33 Great Sutton Street
London EC1V 0DX, UK

www.reaktionbooks.co.uk

First published 2013

Printed and bound in China by C&C Offset Printing Co., Ltd

British Library Cataloguing in Publication Data
Young, Peter, 1930 Sept. 25–
Oak. – (Botanical)
1. Oak. 2. Oak – Mythology.
3. Oak – Folklore.
I. Title II. Series
583.4'6-DC23

ISBN 978 1 78023 037 5

Contents

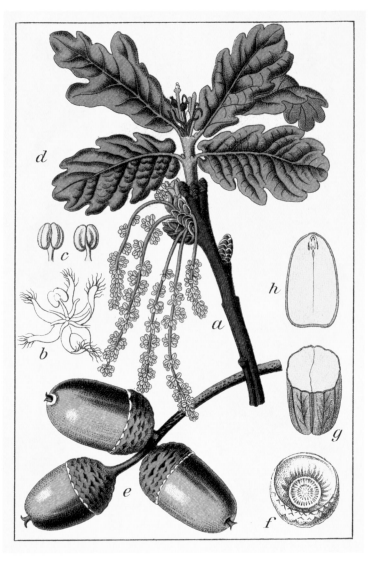

The pedunculate oak (*Quercus robur*) in Jacob Sturm's illustration to Johann Georg Sturm's *Deutschlands Flora in Abbildungen* (1862).

one

Seeing the Trees

༒

To a layman an oak is a tree; to a botanist it is one of a family of trees. While the layman admires a single tree or a group of them in a forest, the botanist enjoys studying their differences. The genus *Quercus* embraces some 600–800 species of hardwood trees and shrubs. It is impossible to be more precise because there are many hybrids, some from the natural fertility of adjacent native oaks, others the work of breeders experimenting with species from distant geographical sources. Among them is one between a Turkey oak (*Quercus cerris*) and a cork oak (*Quercus suber*) from the western Mediterranean. A fast-growing, straight tree reaching as high as 100 ft (30 m), it varies in exhibiting the main characteristics of one of its ancestor species. Some resemble the deciduous Turkey oak, others have a corky bark and evergreen leaves. It adds elegance to parklands but has none of the sturdy qualities commonly associated with oak. Its wood tends to shrink and warp, reducing its use to firewood. Some trees, although so called, are not true oaks. For example, the Australian silky-oak looks like an oak but is about two-thirds the weight of a genuine oak and, though used as a veneer or in steam-bent form, for example in furniture, is not strong or durable enough for outdoor applications.

There are many variations among species. These depend upon the suitability of soils, location and climate, and the diseases to which they are prone. Profiles differ in height and spread, as does the girth of the trunk, appearance and texture of the bark (which changes

Evergreen oak at Westbury Court Gardens in Gloucestershire.

Turkey oak
(*Quercus cerris*).

A mature cork oak (*Q. suber*) in Portugal.

colour over time), size and setting of the acorns, the character of the twigs and stalks, and the shape and colour of the leaves. Their lobes may have rounded or pointed ends, their top and underside subtly different greens. The trees are usually deciduous; the holm oak (*Quercus ilex*), a native of the Mediterranean but introduced to other climates, is an evergreen with pointed leaves. When oak timber is cut, the interior reveals more differences. The weight of the wood reflects its density and porosity. Colours of the timber and regularity of the grain distinguish species. Expert eyes can identify timbers that will dry well, are hard or easy to work and what applications they are suitable for.

Differences between species are the result of their origin and evolution. Forests grew after the melting of the most recent ice sheets: the glaciers withdrew around 10,000 BCE and the landscape of tundra and steppe was gradually transformed. A patchwork of woodland, in places dense, came to cover the plains of Europe, North America and Asia. The types of succeeding forest depended upon latitude, altitude, underlying geology, climate, distance from the sea and other local factors. Wood and tree pollen preserved in peat bogs shows the sequence of types of trees that grew. Oak typically developed after aspen, birch, willow, pine and hazel. Not that there was a rigid division of types of wood: trees grew in mixed forests, for example of oak and ash. Evidence they have left also outlines the rise and fall of different civilizations, as in the Bronze Age culture of southeastern Spain, a dry area of Europe. Pollen sequences show how vegetation changed over thousands of years. An urban society, the Argaric culture, emerged during the third millennium BCE, lasting only some 700 years before disappearing from the archaeological records around 1600 BCE. Originally, it flourished in an area of diverse forest dominated by deciduous oaks and other broad-leaved trees. The presence of significant levels of charcoal in the retrieved pollen sequence points to this natural

Holm oak (*Q. ilex*).

resource being over-exploited. Slash-and-burn cleared the forest for mining and grazing, leaving the ground to grow fire-prone secondary vegetation. Following the transformation of the environment, partly aided by a progressive change to a drier climate, the Argaric civilization disappeared.

Climate change is recorded in tree rings. Under good growth conditions, with plenty of water and nutrients, tree rings are broad and well separated; during a drought rings grow closer together. Data collected from several sites in central Europe has made it possible for personnel at the Swiss Federal Institute for Forest, Snow and Landscape to construct a climate chronology spanning a period of 2,500 years. This has been related to the fortunes of societies, as in the rise, decline and fall of the Roman Empire. Wet and warm summers coincide with periods of prosperity. Conversely, dry summers and marked variations in climate are factors in economic and other

CHÊNE LIÈGE.
Quercus suber. L.

Antiquarian botanical illustrations, such as this elegant depiction of a cork oak
(*Q. suber*), often cross the line between artistic and scientific.

Attractive seeds, acorns symbolically promise many possibilities.

downturns. Climate change was by no means the only cause of the barbarian invasions and the fall of the Roman Empire, but it may well have been a contributory factor.[1] It is also a warning of the kind of long-lasting effects that, at times of global warming, could result from lack of adequate adaptation to a greener way of life.

Different types of oak can grow within comparatively small geographical areas. For instance, there is a difference between 'damp' and 'dry' conditions. 'Dry' was associated with birch or holly and thick but patchy undergrowth; 'damp' with hazel, blackthorn, hawthorn, briars and brambles in dense undergrowth. The pattern of settlement followed accordingly. There was little open country

Anna Johnston, autumn leaves of sessile oak (*Q. petraea*).

until the first farmers began to clear land for raising animals and crops. With only stone tools, it was a slow process. Slash-and-burn, ring barking and grazing could help. Low-lying clay lands were fertile ground for 'damp' oak wood and hence difficult areas in which to create settlements. Well-drained uplands, although they may have had lighter, shallower, less productive soils, were

overleaf: Oaks, Wistman's Wood, Dartmoor.

Bamboo-leaf oak (*Q. myrsinifolia*), one of the *Cyclobalanopsis* sub genus of oak.

places of primary settlement and made for easier communications on paths and trackways. Tackling impenetrable forests with stone and bronze tools was hard work. It was not until the Iron Age, which made the production of strong, cheap and plentiful implements possible, that inroads were made into areas of difficult settlement. Progress in clearing land and establishing wider tracks was not continuous, however. Once cleared, open space had to be

Northern red oak (*Quercus rubra*).

maintained, for whilst not necessarily returning to its previous state, nature was not slow to reassert itself.

Today oak grows in Europe, northern and southern; in the Near East in countries such as Iran; on the lower slopes of the Himalayas and in China and Japan. Canada and the United States have large oak forests. Clearance of land for agriculture has reduced those of Central America, for example in Mexico and sub tropical parts of

With 600–800 species, oaks have many profiles.

northern South America, including the northern Andes. Elsewhere, for instance in the southern hemisphere, a combination of suitable conditions encourages the growth of oak.

With its wide distribution in temperate areas, it is not surprising that many countries and provinces have adopted the oak as their symbol. The tree has accumulated a long and varied history, a wealth of applications and associations. Attitudes have ranged across the spectrum, from concern to passion. It has aroused the pride of patriots, at times had its scarcity bemoaned, and been determinedly destroyed as an emblem of paganism. Neither layman nor botanist though is likely to be aware of the full extent of cultural influence the wood has had: in architecture, beliefs, communications by land and sea and in writing, drinking and eating, the environment, as a resource to be used and conserved, the impact of its scarcity on individual trades and national standing, and much more.

In *Memorials of the Oak Tree* (1863), Isabella Burt wrote of the tree: 'Its chronicles are, to a considerable extent, those of the human

A trunk may be stout and sturdy . . .

An oak may reach upwards . . .

. . . or spread its branches.

race'.[2] Its influence has been basic. Like climate and ocean currents warm and cold, it has been an overall determining factor, a background not always evident. Environment shapes man's history, the farther back in time the more so.

two

Diversity

❦

The reputation of the oak is based not on superlatives but on its character. In human terms it is not a celebrity but a reliable, solid citizen, somebody with integrity. A hardwood, it is regarded as strong and steadfast, majestic, able to withstand the ravages of time. It is mighty but modest, sure of its own stature. So distinctive is its image that the tree is reduced to its extrinsic characteristics when grown in miniature, as a bonsai, a Japanese 'plant in a tray'.

Art may imitate nature, but it is no substitute for the real thing. In his *Life of Samuel Johnson* (1791), James Boswell states that there is nothing like the original, a firm opinion he received in a discussion about Herbert Croft's *Life of Dr Young*:

> It has always appeared to me to have a considerable merit, and to display a pretty successful imitation of Johnson's style. When I mentioned this to a very eminent literary character he opposed me vehemently, exclaiming 'No, no, it is *not* a good imitation of Johnson; it has all his pomp, without his force; it has all the nodosities [knotty swellings] of the oak without its strength; it has all the contortions of the Sibyl without the inspiration.[1]

As befits a tree with a long life, the oak has been sacrosanct for centuries, venerated by diverse believers. In 1861 a comment was made:

Every one knows how many 'Gospel oaks' there are in different places: – the ancient mark trees, distinguishing boundaries, and at which perambulators have, for ages, been accustomed to stand . . . while the 'gospel' has been pronounced, cursing him who moves the landmarks.[2]

Gospel oaks were landmarks at which preachers held forth to their shaded congregations. One in north London has given its name to a suburb and its railway station.

A clergyman sensitive to nature who appreciated the religious significance of the oak tree was the Revd Francis Kilvert (1840–1879), as his diary entry shows for 22 April 1876 describing a country walk in Herefordshire:

We came upon . . . what seemed at first in the dusk to be a great ruined grey tower, but which proved to be the vast ruin of the king oak of Moccas Park, hollow and broken but still alive and vigorous in parts and actually pushing out new shoots and branches. That tree may be 2,000 years old. It measured 33 feet round by arm stretching.

I fear those grey old men of Moccas, those grey, gnarled, low-browed, knock-kneed, bowed, bent, huge, strange, long-armed, deformed, hunchbacked, misshapen oak men that stand waiting and watching century after century, biding God's time with both feet in the grave and yet tiring down and seeing out generation after generation, with such tales to tell, as when they whisper them to each other in the midsummer nights . . . No human hand set those oaks. They are 'the trees which the Lord hath planted'.[3]

In the Old Testament, the oak was a place sacred to believers in the Lord and also to unbelievers, who had their own gods. Under them, faiths were declared and fought for: 'And Joshua wrote these words in the book of the law of God, and took a great stone, and set it up

Etching after Thomas Hearne, *An Oak in Moccas Park, Herefordshire*, 1798.

there under an oak, that was by the sanctuary of the LORD' (Joshua 24:26). In the tribal wars Gideon, the mighty man of valour, received the news that he was to deliver Israel from the Midianites: 'And there came an angel of the LORD, and sat under an oak . . .' (Judges 6:11). A prophet knew the most likely place to end his quest: 'And went after the man of God, and found him sitting under an oak . . .' (Kings 13:14). The Lord God also made his position clear:

> Then shall ye know that I am the LORD, when their slain men shall be among their idols round about their altars, upon every high hill, in all the tops of the mountains, and under every green tree, and under every thick oak, the place where they did offer sweet savour to all their idols. (Ezekiel 6:13)

An oak was also a burial site for the lowly: 'But Deborah Rebekah's nurse died, and she was buried beneath Bethel under an oak . . .' (Genesis 35:8); and of the high: 'They arose, all the valiant men, and took away the body of Saul, and the bodies of his sons, and

brought them to Jabesh, and buried their bones under the oak . . . '
(Chronicles 10:12).

How long does an oak live? In *Urne Burial* (1658) Sir Thomas Browne
(1605–1682) made another comparison with human beings:
'Generations pass while some tree stands, and old families last not
three oaks.' There is an old saying that an oak is 200 years growing,
200 years standing still and 200 years dying. The National Trust in
Britain classes oaks 600 years old as ancient. In 'Palomon and Arcite',
part of *Fables, Ancient and Modern* (1700), poet laureate John Dryden
(1631–1700) went further:

> The monarch oak, the patriarch of the trees,
> Shoots rising up, and spreads by slow degrees.
> Three centuries he grows, and three he stays,
> Supreme in state, and in three more decays.[4]

The times were more fancy than fact. Lifespan depends very much
on the soil in which the tree grows. Oaks are thirsty trees, drawing 60
or more gallons (230 litres) of water a day through their extensive
taproots, from which it rises and evaporates through leaves. They
flourish best in damp soil; conversely, they may struggle on a well-
drained site. Ground conditions make a considerable difference to
their life span. A 'good' soil can enable a tree to live for 500 years, a
'bad' 200 years. Depending upon the species of oak, an acorn containing the seed can take from six to eighteen months to mature.
Thereafter growth is slow and sure, the roots gradually spreading
over a larger surface and penetrating deeper. Again depending upon
the species, the tree will not produce its first good seed crop for 20
to 50 years. In old age growth slows down. Throughout its life the
fate of the oak is in the hands of nature. Its age may be extended by
manual intervention, for example if coppicing is sustained over a
long period to encourage healthy growth.

How do you tell the age of an oak tree? Simply going by appearance is guesswork, as it can be with human beings. The Woodland Trust in the UK has produced a ready reckoner based on the girth of a tree, measured at about one and a half metres from the ground. A tree with a girth of 2 metres (6 ft 7 in.) has an estimated age of 80 years; one of 6.7 m (22 ft 8 in.), 515 years. The estimates are for trees growing in open conditions in the southeast of England, and vary for trees growing under different conditions elsewhere. There are several claims for longevity, and adjudicating them is not easy. Some are estimates, some based in oral tradition, some supposedly linked to a historical event. The Seven Sisters Oak in Lewisburg, Louisiana, is estimated to be 1,000 years old and is considered the largest certified oak tree. Its circumference is 37 ft 2 in. (11.27 m) and its crown spread 150 ft (46 m). When the large Hooker Oak in Chico, California, also estimated to be 1,000 years old, fell in 1977, it was revealed as being two trees that had grown together. Each was 325 years old. In the UK, old Knobbley in Mistley, Essex, is said to be 800 years old, but that may be a local patriotism. The Bull Oak at Wedgnock Park, Warwickshire, was growing at the time of the Norman invasion in 1066. Of a similar period, is Meavy Oak in front of the lychgate of Meavy Church near Yelverton, Devon. Some 25 ft (7.5 m) in circumference, it is reputed to have accommodated nine people sitting down to a meal in its hollow. Reformation Oak on Mousehold Heath on the edge of Norwich in Norfolk was a 'gospel oak' where a new preacher spoke of the newly published Book of Common Prayer in 1549. According to fellow poet Ben Jonson (1572–1637), Sir Philip Sidney's Oak near Penshurst, Kent, was planted at Sidney's birth in 1554, but his descendants believe it is actually a medieval tree under which Sidney sat and wrote pastoral poems. Honour Oak at Whitchurch, Devon, was a boundary marking the limit for French prisoners of war on parole from HM Prison Dartmoor during the Napoleonic War of 1803–15. It was also the place where money was left in exchange for food during the cholera epidemic of 1832.

An old postcard of the 'Hooker Oak' at Chico, California.

At the Baroque Rogalin Palace in western Poland, formerly a seat of the aristocratic Raczyński family and now part of the National Museum of Poznań, the grounds are claimed to have the largest collection of old oaks in Europe. Among some 1,400 trees there are three oaks reputedly 1,000 years old, their boughs supported by crutches. Representing three nations, they are named Lech (Poland), with a circumference of 9.3 m, Czech (Czech Republic), at 8.1 m, and Rus (Russia), 6.7 m. The thickest and oldest tree in Estonia is the Tamme-Lauri oak, planted around 1326. It has been repeatedly struck by lightning and had a cavity big enough for seven standing people. It takes part of its name from the spirit of fire, Laurits, thought to live in the oak (*tamm*) and able to bring good or bad fortune.

The presence of oaks is often evident in place names, which make the tree appear ubiquitous. Obvious examples are Oak Beach, Oak Bluffs, Oak City, Oak Creek, more than one Oakdale, Oak Hill, Oakland (which downtown has Oaksterdam University, founded by an activist in 2007 to offer training 'for the cannabis industry'), and

The Birnam Oak mentioned in Shakespeare's Scottish tragedy *Macbeth*.

Samuel Wale (1721–86), *Robert Kett, under the Oak of Reformation at his Great Camp on Mousehold Heath, Norwich, receives the Earl of Warwick's Herald, 1549. c. 1746.* oil on canvas.

Oakwood all in the USA. Among some 2,500 'company towns' Oak Ridge, Tennessee, hidden from the rest of the world behind barbed-wire fences and elaborate security checks, was unique in being the site where, from 1943, the first atomic bomb was created. Canada has Oak Bay, Oak Island, Oak Point and Oak River; New Zealand an Oakland and Oakleigh, a clearing in an oak wood; Australia Oakbank, Oak Park and Oakvale. Other names such as Burnt Oak, Five Oaks and Sevenoaks in England speak for themselves. County Oak marked a boundary. Oakhurst is an oak hill or wood, Oakreeds land cleared of oaks, and Oakeshott simply a place of oaks. The Old English for oak, *ac,* occurs in a name such as Acton, a *ton* being a hill. Selly Oak is derived from a meadow on a terrace of land, where at one time a landmark oak grew. The Irish *derry* means an oak wood, harking back to the Indo-European linguistic origins of oak in *der* and *derwo,* reflected since 1887 in the Esperanto *kverko.* Dubrovnik's name is derived from the Croatian word meaning 'oak woods', which surrounded the city. In German *Eiche* occurs in several place names, among them Eichberg, Eichendorf, Eichhofen, Eichsfeld, Eichstätt, Eichtersheim and Eichwalde.

Surnames are commonly derived from a place where an ancestor lived, often occurring within a limited geographical area or a few places. Obvious examples are Oakford and Oakhill. An 'Oakden' was an oak valley. Noakes or Nokes, meaning 'at the oak trees', is based on the early Middle English for '*at them* oaks', which became '*atten* oaks', shortened to *'n* oaks. Similarly, Roke stems from *atter,* resulting in 'at the oak'. The Italian word *quercia* occurs in Jacopo della Quercia (*c.* 1374–1438), the sculptor son of a woodcarver who did most of his work in Siena and Bologna and was an influence on Michelangelo. The Flemish painter Jan van Eyck (*c.* 1389–1441) was born probably at Maaseik, i.e. the place of the oaks, on the Maas river. The same sound is heard in the Norse *eik.* An oak village gave its name to the family line of Joseph von Eichendorff (1788–1857), romantic poet and novelist. Similarly, the poet André Chénier (1762–1794) took his name from *chêne* (The French word for oak).

The Rogalin oaks, Poznań, Poland.

One of the most common surnames in Estonia is Tamm, a direct translation of oak. The Finnish equivalent is Tammi. Somewhere in the family tree of Annie Oakley (1860–1926), the American crack shot who appeared in Buffalo Bill's Wild West shows, an ancestor would have lived in part of an oak wood cleared for farming. In ancient China the class of officials appointed to supervise land clearance were called 'men of the oaks'. The tree was an early victim of the spread of agriculture but in the mythic tradition its removal enabled the development of a settled Chinese civilization that in turn brought the prosperity of new technologies and products.[5]

An occupational name or nickname based on an ancestor's appearance and manner can also be evidence of a past link with the tree. Occasionally it seems particularly appropriate to an individual. In Czech, a Slavic language, Dubček means 'little oak' (The Russian word for oak is *dubov*), unfortunately true of Alexander Dubček, who in 1968 tried to create 'socialism with a human face' but was overridden by the Russians. After his downfall he worked for the forestry service.

An enduring legacy of the oak is plain in landmarks and timber-framed buildings that have survived since the Middle Ages. Many are preserved as parts of national heritage, listed according to grades. They cannot be altered without official permission and then only in a very limited way. Old timbers from ruined properties are available to provide a near match to the originals when restoring a listed building. Nevertheless, owners may have to reconcile themselves to the inconvenient fact that, in general, their ancestors were shorter people who were content to live with low doorways and ceilings. Old buildings may at times be impractical, unsuited to the needs and appliances of modern living, but they have the desirable virtue of an irreplaceable character, which commands a premium price.

Like these valuable relics, the oak is often regarded as unique. People who are familiar with only typical images and the few actual examples they have seen can easily see it as *the* tree, their national tree like no other. In fact, within suitable climatic conditions it is ubiquitous and not a stereotype. Native to the northern hemisphere, it is now estimated to amount within the overall genus *Quercus* to some 800 or more species widely distributed in temperate zones and the highlands of some subtropical areas to which it has been introduced: Australasia, Southeast Asia, North and Central America, and Europe. Some species are deciduous, some evergreen, for example the holm oak of Mediterranean origin. An oak is not always a tree; it may be no more than a shrub, even looked upon as scrub to be cleared so that trees can flourish with proper space, light and nutrition. Species are distinguished by physical characteristics not always obvious in the distant profile of a tree or shrub. One needs to take a closer look at details such as leaves, twigs and bark. There is a difference in acorns: while the common oak's acorn, for instance, has a stalk, the sessile oak's has either a very short stalk or none at all. The inside of the acorn, in which the usually single seed is located, can be hairless or appear woolly. Maturity rates of seed vary by species. Different trees are selected for different applications, making them useful for various purposes.

Although called oaks, some commercial hardwoods are not true oaks. For example, Tasmanian oak is the export name for a variety of eucalyptus. Lacking the density of true oak, it is less resistant to decay. Hence it is used in the manufacture of flooring strips, packing cases and, like the Australian silky-oak, in some furniture and joinery.

Moreover, species readily cross-breed naturally. The group of white – as distinct from red – oaks, for instance, easily accept wind-borne pollen. Man-made hybrids are created for specific purposes, usually to combine the desired features of two species, though it is not always possible to eliminate unwanted traits. For example, a decid-uous species, the Turkey oak, was introduced to Britain probably from the Balkans in the early eighteenth century. A fast-growing and straight hardwood, its tall, commanding presence is belied by the quality of its wood, heavy but prone to warping and shrinkage. Hence it is useful for little more than fuel, looking good as a log fire in an inglenook. Several years later, a nurseryman named Lucombe raised a hybrid between the Turkey oak and the cork oak. Named after him,

Sessile oak stools in Banstead Woods, Surrey.

the Lucombe oak has leaves like the Turkey oak and is also more or less evergreen. It is seen at its proud best in open spaces such as parks.[6]

Such variety enables users to select the best species for a particular purpose but it can be a disadvantage when trying to match old oak wood with what is currently available. When at the end of the twentieth century Gonville and Caius College, Cambridge, moved its library from within the college to a nineteenth-century building just across the way, it had a problem with its seventeenth-century bookcases. More space was available and welcome, but it was aesthetically necessary to match the new bookcases as closely as possible with the old ones. The search was worldwide, with Arkansas oak eventually chosen as the best match.

In his essay 'On National Prejudices' Oliver Goldsmith (*c.* 1730–1774) remarks that 'The slender vine twists round the sturdy oak, for no other reason in the world but because it has not strength sufficient to support itself.' The tree is a foster parent to many dependants. Oaks are homes to a diversity of wildlife: animals, birds, insects and plants. Bats and squirrels nest in them; other mammals – badgers, mice, voles – live nearby. Even dead trees are a source of food: many insects living in dead wood are tasty fodder for much of the bird population. The acorns provide sustenance for nut eaters such as chipmunks, field mice, squirrels and other rodents. Having cheek pouches, chipmunks are able to carry more food to their burrows. The animals bury nuts as a store of winter food, then forget or don't find them, and some germinate into seedlings, continuing the natural cycle. This is to the annoyance of gardeners and allotment-holders cultivating ground near oak trees: having deep taproots, the abundant seedlings take time to extirpate. They are also eaten by grazing animals, especially deer, making the survival of a single tree from the several thousands of acorns shed by just one oak in a season a rare outcome. The link is established in German: *Eiche*, an oak;

A chipmunk eating an acorn.

Eichel, an acorn; *Eichhörnchen* or *Eichkätzchen*, a squirrel, a storer of acorns. Jays also collect and bury acorns.

Birds such as flycatchers, nuthatches, tawny owls, tits and wood-peckers build their nests in tree holes, which may be in dead or dying wood that is softer to excavate. The chaffinch hides its family in the crutch of branches, while treecreepers like the shelter of loose bark. Birds of prey, among them buzzards and red kites, choose tall trees such as oaks in which to nest, to give them a wide viewing area. Insect-eating birds such as blackbirds, thrushes and warblers have a varied diet that may include berries, snails and worms. The wood warbler is more limited in its habitat and diet, commonly nesting in the sessile

An oak
titmouse,
a bird native
to North
America.

oak, where it hunts for insects in the treetop. In the same part of the tree, tits feed on moth caterpillars, particularly the winter moth and the green oak moth, which in turn feed on oak leaves. As the leaves grow, they produce bitter-tasting, self-protecting tannin, which toughens them and makes them less digestible. Some 200 species of insects have been found on oaks.

Many species of butterflies and moths depend upon oak trees for food. Notable are the purple emperor butterfly, regarded by naturalists as the 'emperor of the woods', some fritillaries and the speckled wood butterfly. Over 200 species of moths are reckoned to feed on the oak, more than any other European tree. Some have been named after it, for instance the oak beauty, great oak beauty, green oak, oak hook-tip, oak nycteoline and oak-tree pug moths. Colonies of caterpillars can strip foliage from entire branches. Where it survives, caterpillars have to be distinguished from the greenery, and the colouring of moths themselves often affords excellent camouflage against the wood or lichen. Mosses and lichens are among the plants the trees are host to. Oakmoss is unusual among lichens due to its application in perfume manufacture and as a dyeing agent.

Many beetles, of which there are around 250,000 species, are associated with woodland. Their larvae feed on dead or decaying wood, including roots, where they have the company of crickets, earwigs, flies, lice, slugs, snails, centipedes and millipedes. Most notorious is the death watch beetle, the bane of owners of old buildings. A leaking roof can soften timber supporting, making it an easy target. Like woodworm in furniture and household items, the larvae can seriously damage timber. Cash-strapped churches, unable to keep up maintenance, are particularly at risk. Again, some beetles take their name from the tree. The oak bark beetle lives between the outer bark and the inner wood; the red oak roller is a weevil that rolls up a leaf and then lays its eggs inside it so that the larvae can feed in warm security. Nut weevils pierce a hole in an acorn or gall (growths) and then lay their eggs inside.

Various bugs that live by sucking the sap or juices from plants, thrive on oaks. Among them are aphids, which in turn are food for other bugs. More easily seen are species of spiders, the most interesting being the jumping ones (*Salticidae* family). They stalk flies and other prey before finally pouncing on them. On rotting wood beneath oaks or on ground nearby there is a rich variety of fungi. The oak milkcap is an inedible mushroom, and oak mildew is a fungal disease affecting the foliage. A few species of fungi that flourish on the wood of oaks, living or dead, are edible, but not a delicacy. Some cause rot, welcome to beetles that make the wood their home but a nuisance to those who have used it in some form of construction. In the autumn and winter fallen leaves – as many as 100,000 from each tree – are food for a motley contingent of beetles, crickets, mites, shrews, snails, woodlice and earthworms, which return to the soil the vital nutrients – mainly nitrogen, phosphorus and potassium – extracted by the trees in the previous season. Fertility is not lost but, like energy, transformed.

The trees thus have an important role in the ecological cycle, over the seasons preserving the balance of nature in all of its complexity. The oak is more than just a tree. In more than a literal sense it has many roots and branches that grow from it. To try and map the interaction of the abundant life in and around it in accurate detail

Oak milk cap fungi.

would be a major task. The oak is part of a process of growth and decay, creation and destruction, evolved over millennia. Much of it, like a handful of woodland soil containing millions upon millions of bacteria, is unseen. More evident are the many uses man has made of this versatile wood.

three

Home

O ak is a resource. At its simplest, it can be grown as an orna-
mental shade tree. In the form of otherwise unusable
branches and diseased wood, it is a fuel, either as logs in a
cheering fire or as charcoal. As well as producing heat it is a durable
material capable of much more, meeting some of man's other basic
needs. Most visible is shelter. Chaucer (*c.* 1340–1400) called it 'byl-
dere ok' and Edmund Spenser (*c.* 1552–1599) in *The Faerie Queene*
(1590) wrote of 'The builder Oake, sole king of forests all'.[1] In England, under what was known as the 'common of estovers', tenants
had the legal right to use wood from the landlord's estate for repairs
to his property. Whether buildings were for individuals or communities, they were built to last. As a hardwood, oak has a natural
resistance to diseases and pests such as woodworm. Its main enemy
is damp.

Wooden henges ('henge' is derived from the word 'hanging')
may have been man-made imitations of original sacred sites, clumps
of forest trees. We cannot know for certain their purpose. They
may have been built to mark the progress of seasons, important to
farmers, or the setting for cult ceremonies. Whatever their purpose,
they demanded considerable group effort. From the depth of the
postholes at Arminghall near Norwich it is likely that the great oak
posts projected 20 to 30 feet (6–9 m) above ground.[2] Timbers of
this size were probably split rather than cut and trimmed with the
comparatively soft-edged tools of early Bronze Age carpenters. No

evidence of lintels or roofs survives at the timber circles of Wood-henge, near and perhaps a precursor to Stonehenge, and Arminghall: only the pattern of postholes clearly seen as cropmarks in aerial photographs taken in a dry summer. When stonemasons created Stonehenge, they adopted a technique probably devised by prehis-toric carpenters: mortise and tenon joints. Off the north Norfolk coast is Seahenge, a large central oak stump in a rough circle of 55 small spilt oak trunks, felled according to dendrochronology (tree-ring dating) in 2049 BCE. This may have been a mortuary enclosure rather than a henge.

Split logs secured by wooden tongues were also used as uprights in early Christian churches such as the late tenth-century Cathedral of St Sophia in Novgorod, Russia, and in the mid-eleventh-century parish church at Greensted, Essex. Outsize timbers were particularly useful in church towers. In the thirteenth century Henry III provided oaks from royal forests for church building, cathedral roofs and castles all over his kingdom. The timber was also used in reclaiming water-logged land, as the Dutch did in Amsterdam from the late twelfth century, and for underpinning large buildings on soft soils. Notable

The remains of Seahenge off Huntstanton, Norfolk.

The oak walls of the Church of St Andrew, Greensted-juxta-Ongar, Essex.

was Winchester Cathedral, the Norman oak foundations of which had become waterlogged and subsided by the early twentieth century, threatening the collapse of parts of the building. From 1905 to 1912, led by a diver, William Walker, a team underpinned the cathedral with concrete. The extent of their work is conveyed by the amount of material needed: 25,000 bags of concrete; 115,000 concrete blocks; 900,000 bricks. At times shoring up a building over 800 years old involved working at depths up to 20 ft (6 m) in total darkness.

It was simpler to build chapels within oaks, as the French did. At Allouville-Bellefosse in Seine-Maritime is the 15-m-high (50-ft) Chêne Chapelle (chapel oak) between 800 and 1,200 years old, with a circumference of 16 m at the base. Its hollow trunk contains two chapels built in 1669: Notre Dame de la Paix (Our Lady of Peace), to which there is a pilgrimage on 15 August, the feast of the Assumption, and Chambre de l'Ermite (Hermit's Room). Entry to both chapels is via a spiral staircase around the trunk. There are also chapel oaks in Saint-Sulpice-le-Verdon, Vendée, and in Villedieu-la-Blouère, Maine-et-Loire.

Chêne Chapelle. Allouville-Bellefosse. near Rouen. Normandy

Medieval timber-framed buildings have lasted: homes of the prosperous few, halls of castles, colleges and inns. These were prefabricated and the structures tested off-site, the individual timbers with their fixing holes being identified by carpenters' marks based on Roman numerals. Not all timbers were straight; naturally curved timbers, or crucks, were employed as bracing. On site, the frame was erected either on a sole plate, a large oak beam or a stone foundation. Pegs secured the joints. Cut from fresh oak, which was easier to work than seasoned timber, the structure dried out and tightened. If the timber was too green, however, in shrinking it could twist and distort the load-bearing frame, cracking the infilling as well. Space between uprights was filled with wattle and daub or lath and plaster, later superseded by more watertight brick. Similarly, safer stone and tile roofs succeeded thatched roofs. Oak was not an inferior substitute for stone afforded by the rich; a material of choice, it had its own natural qualities, was architecturally pleasing and said something about its owner. A larger than average farmhouse, for instance, was made of some 330 small trees.[3] Single-storey buildings developed into two storeys or even more, floors sometimes jettying out above the one below. An outstanding example is Pattyndenne Manor, built in the fifteenth century near Goudhurst, Kent, which has external corner posts of upturned oaks.

Methods of timber-frame construction were so well established that they were taken to the New World in the seventeenth century by the early European settlers, who found suitable wood aplenty. The tradition of building in wood became well established and continues today. Surviving early buildings now form part of American heritage. The oldest remaining one, built in around 1637, is Fairbanks House, Dedham, Massachusetts. Indeed, there was a tradition that oak was imported from England and stored in Boston before being transported to Dedham. In Williamsburg, colonial capital of Virginia, the eighteenth-century houses have been restored and are a major tourist attraction. Especially among religious groups such as the Amish and the Shakers, raising a timber-framed house was often a community activity. For newlyweds, an assured roof over their heads was a welcome start to married life. As American society became mobile, one of the attractions of a timber-framed house was that it could be dismantled and transported to another site. Others are still being built, not just as replicas.

For an American architect of marked originality, Frank Lloyd Wright (1869–1959), the affinity of art and nature developed into a philosophy that he passed on to younger generations of architects. Having worked under Louis H. Sullivan (1856–1924), a pioneer of skyscrapers who believed that form should express function, Wright went on to design something on a different plane: long, low houses with the emphasis on horizontal lines. Known as prairie houses, many of them were designed for clients in Oak Park, Illinois, a Chicago suburb, where he had a studio. His guiding principle, as seen for instance in the William E. Martin House, built in 1903, was that the constructed environment should be an integral part of its natural environment: 'The good building is not one that hurts the landscape, but one which makes the landscape more beautiful than it was before the building was built.' Following this precept did not have to entail expense; it is more a case of imagination responding to sensitivity. In planning a working farm for C. Leigh Stevens in Yemassee, South Carolina, Wright set the walls of buildings, made of native cypress, at 80° rather than the usual 90° to echo the oak trees on the property.[4] Moreover, buildings strongly influence the people who live and work in them, so the layout and furnishings of the interior are all part of Wright's design. Although he worked on urban buildings such as churches, office blocks, hotels and the Guggenheim Museum in New York, he believed in bringing people 'back to nature', going so far as to incorporate natural features of the landscape into houses: the outstanding example being Fallingwater, a house cantilevered over a waterfall.

In recent years, builders have gone beyond this, building houses within trees for holidaymakers who want to 'get away from it all' and try something different. It is turning away from manufactured products – brick, concrete, steel – which could have come from anywhere, to traditional natural materials that have an association with the place in which they are used. Positively, it is an attempt, however brief, to get closer to nature in the spirit of the New England naturalist and philosopher Henry David Thoreau (1817–1862), but less intensely.

In 1846 he made a study trip to the Maine Woods and published essays under that title in two years later:

> Talk of mysteries – Think of life in nature, – daily to be shown matter, to come into contact with it, rocks, trees, wind on our cheeks! The solid earth! The natural world! The common sense! Contact! Contact! Who are we? Where are we?[5]

Like Thoreau, developers have established their unusual real estate within easy reach of apparent wilderness and human habitation. In Britain, Forest Holidays has built log cabins and treehouses on Forestry Commission land such as England's largest oak woodland, the Forest of Dean. In Sherwood Forest, Center Parcs has built luxury treehouses with smoked oak timber walls and oak-planked floor, complete with 42 inch plasma TVs and iPod docks throughout. Treehouses at other resorts in Europe and Latin America give visitors the impression of being close to nature, having a room wrapped round a tree or with branches protruding into the living space. External appearance in the form of a fairytale cottage or a large bird's nest may add to the fantasy. The illusion can be shattered on closer inspection, when discovering the means of access: an electronic stepladder descending and retracting on the operation of a keypad attached to a tree.

Modern timber-framed houses that are environmentally conscious in a broader sense are becoming more common. In Cambridgeshire a carpenter, Kelly Neville, and his wife Masako, have built an eco-home on their smallholding for a self-sufficient and indeed comfortable way of life. They grow their own food. Energy comes from a wind turbine and fuel of coppiced willow. Heat is conserved by straw bale insulation. Rainwater is filtered and waste products treated naturally, to return to the land. Their two-storey oak-framed house reflects shapes in the natural world, in being hexagonal. One of the pure forms of the ancient Greeks, a hexagon, as in the cross-section of a honeycomb, is not only structurally strong but provides the most storage within the available space. Inspired by J.R.R. Tolkien's *The Hobbit*, the interior is built round a vyse, a spiral staircase carved from an 800-year-old oak tree trunk. Natural light is maximized by large windows and a roof lantern above the staircase. The house sits on stilts, minimizing the risk of flooding from the Fens. Across the flat fen there is a view of Ely Cathedral, described by the historian G. M. Trevelyan as 'floating like an ark upon the waters'.[6] Its central Octagon surmounted by the 'Lantern Tower', built about 1330, is probably the grandest timber structure ever built in England.

A potential limiting factor for aristocrats wanting the prestige of a great hall for their grand receptions, and institutions such as colleges and companies needing a wide hall for their gatherings, was the safe span of the arch supporting the roof timbers. The simple and visually attractive medieval solution was the hammer-beam roof. Short horizontal beams known as hammers, supported by wall posts and curved braces, projected from the wall. They thus reduced the span of the main arch and made a much broader floor area possible without any intrusive intermediate upright. This type of construction, sturdy enough to support the main arch, also encouraged carving of the functional hammer ends in the form of angels, shields, fruits or lanterns. Carpenters and carvers, using timber for different purposes, had to choose their oak carefully. Some is slow-grown, some fast-grown. Slow-grown oak is lighter, comparatively low in strength, but easily worked. Fast-grown oak is heavier, more robust and harder to work. Hammer-beam roofs on the scale of buildings such as the four-teenth-century Westminster Hall in the House of Parliament were striking enough to make first-time visitors look aloft in admiration.

In large private houses, a central feature attracting the attention of visitors in Elizabethan times was the carved oak staircase. At Hatfield House, Hertfordshire, home of Robert Cecil, the style is that of the Italian Renaissance, elaborately carved with a figure standing on each newel. Earlier, intricately carved staircases rising to a pulpit existed in mosques. From the tenth to the fifteenth century, working with basic tools, Egyptian woodcarvers patiently produced intricate

The hammer-beam roof, Westminster Hall, Houses of Parliament, London.

work, treating wood as a precious material, in part because it was scarce locally and had to be imported. Many small panels were used to cover a large area and the lattice grilles that served as windows in Arab houses consisted of tiny, loosely fitting balls and sockets that while diffusing strong sunlight, allowed for warping. Some of the craftsmen's finest work can be seen in the Ibn Tulun Mosque in Cairo (1296), a prime example of the use of Turkey oak.[7]

47

In Christian churches, the work of carvers is evident in screens and on misericords, the shelves on the underside of seats that tipped up and relieved choristers from the pain of standing during a long service: they could appear to be standing when they were in fact sitting. The medieval carvings on these blocks of oak, only seen when the seat is raised, are not necessarily religious. Secular, even pagan, subjects are featured, often outnumbering the sacred. A common decoration was a central motif, often a family coat of arms or an animal, supported by oak leaves and acorns. Scenes from folklore and fables, domestic tasks and disputes, fantastic creatures, the bawdy and the satirical all meant something in an age when the sacred and the profane appeared alongside one another. For most of the year common folk would have been excluded from the inner sanctum of the choir, but on certain feast days they would have been permitted to see and enjoy everyday subjects they understood and wonder about creatures beyond their ken. Carving was not the end of decoration. Just as walls were often painted with holy scenes to tell biblical stories to an illiterate congregation, wood was coloured or gilded to create a bright atmosphere contrasting with the dull daily surroundings of humble dwellings.

A Green Man in church decoration in Poitiers, France.

Sitting on thick, low oak benches, sometimes with carved ornaments, and looking up to gilded angels mounted against a bright blue roof, parishioners felt they had a foresight of their next life. Out of sight in the tower was the substantial oak bell frame, though in modern installations oak has been superseded by cast iron and steel.

The Church had a hand in commissioning another important type of medieval building: the storage barn. Two of the most spectacular European examples survive in Essex, at Cressing Temple. They were the responsibility of the Knights Templar, an order of warrior-monks founded to protect pilgrims travelling to the Holy Land that grew into a powerful wealthy organization owning estates across the Continent. Both of the English oak barns date from the thirteenth century: the barley barn, an aisled structure like a church, from around 1205–35, is believed to be the oldest timber-framed barn in the world. The wheat barn, which with its soaring timbers has been likened to a cathedral, was erected about 50 years later. Both barns were refurbished towards the end of the twentieth century.

A more famous reconstruction was that of Shakespeare's 'wooden O', the Globe Theatre, on a one acre site on the south bank of the River Thames. It was the fulfilment of a sustained effort by the American actor-director Sam Wanamaker, who was surprised that London lacked a permanent recognition of the nation's greatest dramatist, a man whose reputation has grown worldwide during the past 400 years. Wanamaker's own effort from conception to culmination took nearly 50 years, and by the time the Globe was opened he had been dead for four. There were no building records of the original oak-framed building of 1599, so the reconstruction was based on contemporary references, notably the £440 contract for building the Fortune Theatre dated 8 January 1600. In detailing the elements of the construction, layout, dimensions and facilities of the Fortune, references are made to 'the late erected playhouse on the Bank . . . called the Globe', concluding that the Fortune should be 'in all other contrivitions, conveyances, fashions, thing and things effected, finished and done, according to the manner and fashion of the said house called the Globe'.[8]

The result of using the timber of more than 1,000 English oaks was a perimeter seating over 1,000 spectators in three covered galleries, with standing room for 500 'groundlings' in the centre, open to the air. As with other timber-framed buildings, fabrication was done off-site, by the specialist firm McCurdy & Co. To ensure that all the timbers would fit together perfectly on-site, great care had to be taken with the level of the foundations: a concrete base, replica brick plinths and sills for the timber. On-site erection and finishing, punctuated by funding and other delays, was spread over ten years. As the original Globe Theatre had burned down after only fourteen years, when a spark from a cannon used in a performance ignited the thatched roof, there was considerable debate about fire safety measures. This was the first major building with a thatched roof to be built in Central London since the Great Fire of 1666. Satisfying the fire authorities required some design modifications.[9]

The design of an Elizabethan theatre was based on the layout of a typical inn, of which there were several nearby in Southwark below London Bridge, the only means into the City from the south. The best-known was the Tabard Inn, where Chaucer's pilgrims assembled for their journey to Canterbury in the late fourteenth century. As shown in a nineteenth-century engraving, travellers entered from the road through a gateway. Around the courtyard were stables with galleried accommodation above. Repairs to the Tabard during Elizabeth I's reign included the use of oak panels. Panelling, sometimes elaborately carved, was used frequently in large country houses, especially in long galleries, the room in which one could take a winter walk indoors, combining exercise with contemplation of family portraits. A more vigorous exercise was dancing and children could also play there. If fireplaces existed, usually in the centre or one at each end of a gallery, their warmth had limited reach, prompting either more clothing or a brisk walk.

Outside, oak was a security material. In castles and at the entrance to fortified towns it was used for drawbridges. An additional defence was the heavy portcullis, spiked at the bottom and suspended by chains. Operated by a counterweight, it could be lowered quickly in the event of an assault. Such defensive installations have lasted for longer and better than comparable modern items, becoming attractions in the heritage industry. At the same time, as more settled conditions prevailed, timber had a more modest role as material for fencing and gates. A peaceful use of oak was the construction of an aviary at Kenilworth Castle, Warwickshire, for the last visit of Elizabeth I. Her visit in 1575, to see her great love Robert Dudley, Earl of Leicester, lasted only nineteen days. The aviary and the Elizabethan garden have been restored, which took longer than the original work.

Inside, an oak floor does not have to mean thick sturdy boards; it can be elegant, perhaps in parquet or sprung for a ballroom. The first such floor in Europe was opened with the first dance by King Edward VII at The Grand in Folkestone, Kent in 1909. One way in which American heads of state put their stamp on the presidency is by having the decor of the Oval Office changed. In 1982, Ronald Reagan had the wood-grain linoleum of Lyndon B. Johnson's administration replaced with white pine and oak parquet. George W. Bush had this changed in 2005 to a pattern of walnut and oak.

Among other species of wood, ancient Greek and Roman carpenters used oak for furniture, but not much survives. Some can be seen on decorated pottery; actual pieces were preserved by accident. Pompeii, buried by the eruption of Vesuvius in 79 CE, is an example. One gets the impression that homes in the classical world were sparsely furnished, the main items consisting of beds, couches, chairs and stools.

It is from the Middle Ages that we have the most evidence of everyday craftsmanship. Small tables, for instance, were made in two parts, a base and top. Though still heavy, these could be taken apart to make space in the main room for other activities. Some oak tables from the fourteenth century have lasted, and can still be used today. Also serving as a table, the common chest was both storage space and seat. Another dual-purpose construction was a chair-table, in which the back of the chair could be quickly adjusted to provide an attached table. Chests for the safekeeping of valuables, which could include documents, were deliberately of heavy construction, even being hollowed out from a solid baulk of timber, to make their theft more difficult. Partly as a deterrent, mortuary chests containing the bones of Saxon kings were kept high up in Winchester Cathedral. After a fire in the late twelfth century destroyed much of Glastonbury Abbey, two oak coffins were discovered below the ground containing the bones of a large man with a skull wound and a woman with traces of yellow hair, thought to be the sixth-century remains of King Arthur and Queen Guinevere. They were reinterred in Glastonbury Abbey on the orders of Edward I (1239–1307).

One of the items chosen by the British Museum and included in *A History of the World in 100 Objects* broadcast on BBC Radio 4 in 2010 was an example of peasant art, a fifteenth-century iron-bound Flemish carved oak coffer thought to have been a box for women's finery. Chairs – boxy items possessed only by the wealthy – had storage space under the seat. Most people had to be content with rougher-made benches, stools and boxes. Finer finishes, perhaps with carving, were for altars, a specialised form of table. A massive communal table, like the high table in the hall of Middle Temple, one of the Inns of Court in the City of London, had to be made *in situ*. This example consists of three 29-ft (9-m) planks cut from a single oak. Reputedly a gift from Elizabeth I, these were cut down in Windsor Forest and floated down the Thames for installation before the building was even complete. Below it stood another table, the 'cup-board' made from the hatch cover of Sir Francis Drake's ship the *Golden Hind*. The Round Table in the Great Hall of Winchester Castle, made of English oak and dated to the thirteenth century and not

Two in one: The back of the late-17th-century chair folds down to create a table.

the Dark Ages, has nothing to do with the legendary king and his Knights of the Round Table. One suggestion is that the real Round Table may not have been a piece of colourful furniture at all but a stone and wood structure within the Roman amphitheatre at Chester, suitable for a mass gathering.[10]

The world's most famous oak desk, at which the US president makes his decisions, is appropriately called the Resolute desk. President Harry S. Truman had a notice on it that read:'The buck stops here.' It was presented in 1880 to President Rutherford B. Hayes by Queen Victoria, who asked for timbers from the Arctic exploration ship HMS *Resolute* to be reused and made into desks. *Resolute* was one of five ships that in 1852 went in search of Sir John Franklin, who in 1845 had embarked from Britain to find the Northwest Passage through the Canadian Arctic. The rescue was as futile as the original expedition; *Resolute* had to be abandoned in the pack ice. By 1855 she had drifted 1,200 miles (2,000 km). An American whaler saw her adrift and sailed her to New London, Connecticut. She was refurbished and sailed back to Britain, where she was presented as a gift to Queen Victoria in a gesture of peace and friendship. Using her for another search in the Canadian Arctic was pointless, in 1879 she was broken up. American presidents have used the *Resolute* desk in various parts of the White House. Since 1960, when Jackie Kennedy had it moved into the Oval Office, its fame has grown. Replicas of it have been made for museums and use in films. In the action-adventure film *National Treasure: Book of Secrets* (2007), the *Resolute* desk led the treasure-hunting hero to the president's book that gave the clues to the whereabouts of the hidden city of gold. Its discovery was a matter of family honour, proving that his ancestors were not involved in the assassination of Abraham Lincoln.

Beds were once a major item of furniture. The wealthy could afford four-posters, stained and sometimes also brightly painted. An alternative to staining was using fumed oak, timber exposed to ammonia, which turns the golden wood dark. Elaborate carvings added distinction along with decorative hangings, which also served to keep out

The Great Bed of Ware carved in oak, late 16th century.

draughts. An outstanding Elizabethan example is the Great Bed of Ware, originally made for a Hertfordshire inn, and over the centuries many of its users carved their names in its oak posts. Measuring 10 x 11 ft (3 m²), it could accommodate fifteen people.

Near the end of Shakespeare's will occurs 'Item, I give unto my wife my second-best bed, with the furniture'. Was the bed inferior because it was not made of oak? Beds have strong personal meanings: 'I do miss my own bed'. Places where we spend about a third of our lives, they are more than items of furniture. At their best they are associated with relaxation, contemplation, inspiration, creation and love. Historically, major items of furniture such as beds and dressers were treated with oil to seal the grain and protect the surface. Made to last and carefully maintained, items acquired associations and appreciated in value, not least because they became heirlooms. Handing furniture down for later generations was a practical way of signalling continuity within a family.

If you did not have a source within the family, the simple solution was to buy. This was the case for the American writer Mark Twain (1835–1910), who in 1873 visited Ayton Castle, Berwickshire, where he insisted on buying the ornate dining-room fireplace, an item of Victorian sumptuosity. Made of carved oak, the mantel suited the Scottish Baronial style in which the castle had been built in 1851. Twain had it installed in the library of the three-storey house he was building in Hartford, Connecticut. The fireplace, rather than his books, dominated the room. In 1878 in Venice he bought a heavy Italian bed made of dark walnut, for his master bedroom. The headboard was carved in a bas-relief of cupids, nymphs and seraphs, the six-winged angels said to guard the Throne of God. Rather than have it behind him, Twain put his pillows at the foot of the bed and slept backwards, so that this heavenly vision of success would be the first thing he saw every day when he woke. In his favourite bed he smoked a pipe or cigar and wrote, eventually dying in it.

Basic agricultural tools such as shovels, needing little attention to detail, could be made in poor light in winter, when work on the land was limited. Outdoors, with the help of a piece of oak and a pole lathe, humble folk could turn out small but treasured items such as bowls, cups, pestles and mortars, platters and spoons. A particular type of spoon, the love spoon, was carved. The practice is associated with Wales, but the tradition existed in parts of Europe and in Africa, from Algeria to Mozambique. It probably developed from the making of wooden spoons for everyday use such as for serving stew. They carried the associations of food, family life and sharing and are also items that fit neatly together. People who had little could not afford expensive presents but they were not poor in imagination. Shy, young men would express their feelings through love tokens. From one piece of oak they carved love spoons, a personal gift as a sign of interest or even devotion. Working with simple tools, sometimes no more than a penknife, made it a long job. The size and intricacy of the finished token could be taken as a measure of the carver's affection. If the girl accepted his gift, they could be in a relationship. This tradition could be the origin of the term 'spooning', the sentimental behaviour of young lovers to one another. Love spoons, carved with symbols, were often hung on the wall as mementos. Motifs included obvious ones such as a heart for love, a horseshoe for luck, as well as various representations of togetherness: chain, knot, ring, twisted stem. A key or lock meant security and oak leaves were a sign that love grows. In Wales symbols were translated into the flowing lines of Celtic heritage.

In recent decades, as part of the growing concern for conservation, there has been an increased interest in traditional crafts. The purpose of the Tools and Trades History Society (TATHS), formed in the UK in 1983, is to ensure the preservation of hand tools, many unique, made or adapted by individuals before the days of mass production. A simple example that survives in a craft that continues today only for the tourist trade, and found in folk museums is a homemade device for crushing raw flax. Many crafts were superseded, but their artefacts and the knowledge that went with them do not have to be consigned to the dustbin of history. Traditionally woodworking tools included such items as adzes, axes, planes, shave horses and spokeshaves. Today tungsten-tipped tools are often used for working with oak. Whether the implements are traditional or modern there is the creative satisfaction of involvement in a personal craft. As one carver put it: 'There's no wood like oak to work with. It has a smell all of its own.'

One man who returned to using traditional craft tools in the twentieth century, especially adzes that create surfaces of gentle waves, was Robert Thompson (1876–1955). The son of the village carpenter, joiner and wheelwright in Kilburn, North Yorkshire, and inspired by the Arts and Crafts movement of William Morris, he developed a business there in carving and joinery using only naturally seasoned English oak. A chance remark by one of his craftsmen in 1919 about 'being as poor as church mice' led him to carve a mouse on a church screen he was working on. It became his trademark, registered in the 1930s, and he became known as the Mouseman of Kilburn. He produced furniture for schools and churches, and smaller items such as napkin rings and cheeseboards for individuals, all but his earlier work bearing a carved mouse symbol. Today every craftsman in his workshop carves his own signature mouse in what is still a family business.

The purpose of the Association of Polelathe Turners and Greenwood Workers (1990), small and British-based but international in its outlook, is to further the practice of woodturning, a skill that originated around the early Middle Ages. Revival of the skill has been promoted by members running courses, exchanging information through meetings, their own journals and newsletters, and demonstrations at country shows. Setting up a pole lathe is not expensive and can be done quickly. It does not need a power source other than a human foot operating a treadle. Its essential elements are a frame, often in oak, a flexible pole acting as a spring, a cord and a spindle. A chisel is the cutting edge used to turn round objects: candlesticks, chair legs, tool handles and so on, while gouges produce bowls. There are also many local clubs.

The bounty of the oak extends to food and drink. Wild boar and farmed pigs eat acorns, free food for the taking, although sometimes the practice has been subject to restrictions, as under the feudal system. Although commoners had pannage, the right or privilege to pasture swine, it was within rules as set by the lord of the manor. For example, full-grown pigs might be permitted to be turned out only if their noses were ringed to restrain them from rooting. They could only eat wind-blown acorns because it was against the rules to shake the trees. The variety of oak affects the taste of the pork. In Portugal and Spain herds of Alentejano (black Iberian) pigs, shorter and fatter than white north European breeds, forage for acorns of the cork and holm oak, the evergreen oak of the Mediterranean region. These acorns impart a distinctive flavour to Serrano hams and the spiced sausage, *chorizo*, often used as a casserole meat. The pigs can shelter from the sun under the spreading flat-topped canopy of the holm oak, the roots of which promote the growth of truffles. In a virtuous circle of nature, eager pigs – to which truffles smell like a sow in heat – detect the valuable underground fungi in truffle orchards or 'truffieres'.

Wood pigeons can consume over 100 acorns a day and carry some in their crops. As well as eating acorns, deer browse on oak leaves. When a tree is pollarded, i.e. cut back to produce a close growth of young branches forming a round canopy, the removed foliage can be stored for use in winter as animal feed. Tree fodder, a renewable resource sometimes referred to as 'leaf hay', probably pre-dates the use of hay and the development of the scythe. Acorns can be put out as bait for catching small animals. In turn, the animals become part of the food chain. Foods like bacon, ham and fish are traditionally flavoured and preserved by being smoked in vertical ovens over oak chippings and sawdust, by-products of trades such as furniture making and boat building. Herrings, for example, take eighteen to twenty hours in a smoker to become kippers. In the past this practice was essential for winter food availability and hence big business. In his *Tour Through the Whole Island of Great Britain* (1724–6), Daniel Defoe records:

> At Halifax, Leeds and other great manufacturing Towns, and adjacent to these, for the two months of September and October, a prodigious Quantity of Black Cattle is sold.
>
> This demand for Beef is occasioned thus: the usage of the People is to buy in at that season Beef sufficient for the whole Year which they kill and salt, and hang up in the smoke to dry. This way of curing their Beef keeps it all the Winter, and they eat the smoaked [sic] Beef as a very great Rarity.'[11]

Silkworms usually feed on leaves from the mulberry tree, but an alternative host is the Japanese oak, which can take to soils where the mulberry does not grow so easily. Thus it is possible to produce high-quality Japanese silk outside Japan. Similarly, silkworms have been found to consume both Chinese oak and American red oak leaves. Intake affects the output: for instance, since Himalayan silk is coarse it is suitable for furnishings and interiors, rather than elegant clothing.

The nutmeat of acorns can be roasted and ground to produce a kind of coffee, ersatz in wartime, and perhaps an unfortunate necessity in peacetime austerity. The ancient Greeks and the people of prehistoric Japan were only too ready to take advantage of nature's bounty. For some, when harvests failed and famine loomed, falling back on foraged food was a matter of survival. Native Americans steeped acorns in water, preferably running, to remove the bitter tannin before grinding the nutmeat into flour that was used for staples such as bread, porridge and the long-lasting, nutritious cake pemmican. Koreans make acorn jelly, *dotorimuk*, and acorn noodles. Lovers of the simple life and healthy living point to the advantages of eating acorns: the fruit is free for the picking and examination to detect fungal diseases or penetration by insects is easy; it can be stored; it is rich in nutrients and minerals; low in sugar content, therefore good for maintaining blood sugar levels; lower in saturated fats than most other nuts; and is gluten-free. As well as being an ingredient in baked items such as bread, cakes, muffins and tortillas, acorn flour is used as a thickening agent for soups and stews. As with any other food, care has to be taken in choosing the ingredient. Acorns from red oaks contain more tannin than those from white oaks, and have to be soaked and the nut meat dried in an oven or the sun before use.

Oaks are hosts to edible fungi that grow as fan-shaped brackets on the trunk, often in the form of a stack. Best known is 'chicken of the woods', so called because its flaky white flesh tastes like chicken breast. Ideally it should be harvested in late summer, when it is a bright yellow growth so striking one might think it poisonous. The older the fungus gets the tougher the texture and the taste can be sour. It should be carefully cut off close to the tree so that it will regenerate for the next season; the younger growth is tastiest. It can be added to a simple omelette or served breaded, with wild garlic and walnut mayonnaise. Found in Australia, Europe, North Africa and North America is beefsteak fungus, also known as 'ox tongue' due to its red colour and propensity to 'bleed' like raw meat. More time has to be taken over preparation of this nourishing mushroom to remove the tannic acid that mars the taste. Methods include soaking in milk, and parboiling. Cutting into small strips before grilling ensures more thorough cooking of what can be coarse to the palate.

White charcoal (*bincho-tan*), made from oak, is used in traditional Japanese cooking. Skewered meat, vegetables and seafood is grilled over its embers because it does not smoke or give off unpleasant odours that could spoil the taste of food. Its production dates back to the Edo period (1603–1868), and is made from a particular species of oak, *ubame*, which burns at a lower temperature than black charcoal and for longer. Moreover, being very porous, pieces of it can be added to rice during cooking to absorb any chalky flavour. For the same reason, it can be used as an air freshener.

Oak leaves, picked at a time of the year to suit taste, are the main ingredient of a homemade wine. Other ingredients are few: sugar, lemon juice, nutrient to promote healthy growth of the active elements, yeast and water. The process of fermentation is simple.

Medicinal uses of oak pre-date proprietary products of the pharmaceutical industry. Based on tribal and traditional remedies, they have survived in alternative or holistic medicine and are now well documented in a growing number of articles and books. Tannin, the astringent chemical in oak bark, has internal and external applications. A decoction or tincture is taken internally, and sparingly, to treat diarrhoea and dysentery. Acorn powder, added to wine, acts as a diuretic, increasing urine flow. Tannin can also be used as a mouthwash for bleeding gums or gargled to ease the inflammation of a sore throat. A decoction of acorns and oak bark with milk is believed to be an antidote to some poisonous herbs. Gallic acid from oak galls has been injected for use against the venereal disease gonorrhoea and the female affliction 'the whites', leucorrhoea. Used externally, it is an antiseptic that can be used in a cream or ointment for the healing of abrasions, cuts, eczema and haemorrhoids. Oak-derived remedies are listed by the Greek physician Dioscorides (first century CE) in *De Materia medica,* a book that superseded all other books on pharmacology and became the standard work for centuries in the East and West. Galen (*c.* 130–201 CE) applied bruised oak leaves to heal wounds. Powdered bark is inhaled in the form of snuff for dealing with nasal polyps and the early stages of some lung diseases. Oak lungs, a lichen found growing on oaks, was also used to treat diseases of the lungs. Tanners, using tannin in their work, were reputed to suffer less from these, just as milkmaids were protected against smallpox by working with cattle. Oak, another lichen growing on oaks, is used as an ingredient in perfume.

In any discussion of its applications it has to be remembered that oak is not just one wood. There are many species and much depends on where and how they are grown, which affects their technical properties. For instance, if white oak is grown quickly it has a dense, tough character, making it hard to work but providing a durable timber. In contrast, slowly grown white oak trees are lighter in weight, easier to work, but not as strong. Red oak is heavier but less durable than white oak. Because it distorts, evergreen oak is not easily dried to produce a usable timber; application is limited to rough woodwork or as a fuel.

With the variety of choice in material and its expected life, users have to be sure of their application requirements. This is even truer of uses outside the home. In the wider world oak has many more specialized applications, each one having to be durable and reliable because performance of the timber affects more people at any one time. Whether it is a means of transport, an engineering component or part of belief system, it can be a factor in determining the destiny of nations.

A reconstruction of one of the Bronze Age boats found at Ferriby, Yorkshire.

four
Away
❦

In one of his *Odes*, the Roman poet Horace (65–8 BCE) wrote: 'His breast must have been protected all round with oak and three-ply bronze, who first launched his frail boat on the rough sea.'[1] The first boats, dating from the Middle Stone Age, were dug-out canoes propelled and guided by a paddle, probably plying the relative calm and shelter of lakes and rivers. Dug-out canoes, created by gouging rather than building, have a similar design to coffins. It was a simple process: an oak trunk split horizontally made a coffin and lid, or two boats. Rounding the ends for a smoother passage through water was a refinement. Sometimes a boat served a dual purpose, as in the boat burials of people who had a leading role in their community. This is likely due to a belief in a voyage to the next world.[2] A change in the dug-out method of construction was discovered in three boats found on the north shore of the River Humber at Ferriby, East Yorkshire. All three, dated to the Early Bronze Age, were built of oak planks 3–4 inches (7.5–10 cm) thick, sewn together with twisted yew branches. Of the same construction was a boat found at Dover dating from 1575–1520 BCE, where it was possibly involved in cross-Channel trade.

Rich in woods such as cedar and fir, the Mediterranean world reserved oak for the frames of ships to make the hull rigid. In northwest Europe cargo ships such as the Gallo-Roman one dating from the late first or early second century CE, discovered in a harbour of the Channel island Guernsey, were constructed entirely of oak. With

The Oseberg ship, Norway.

A replica of the Oseberg ship has been built at Tonsberg, Norway, near where the original was buried as part of a ceremony for the Norse fertility goddess Froya. Viking detail has been retained in the carved keel.

an estimated 40 timber frames, it was a substantial flat-bottomed sailing ship 80 ft (25 m) long and having a maximum beam of some 20 ft (6 m). Whatever the belief behind it, ship burial was still practised in the early seventh century CE. At Sutton Hoo in East Anglia a 90-foot-long seagoing oak boat of considerable but unknown weight was hauled up from the River Deben to the brow of a hill 100 ft higher and lowered into a trench. In the burial chamber of the boat were rich grave goods, including gold and silverware, from Gaul, the Mediterranean area and evidencing some Norse influence. The occupant was probably an Anglo-Saxon king.

Ship burial was practised by the Vikings. Tree-ring dating of the Oseberg ship, built in Norway almost entirely of oak, gives a burial date of 834 CE. Over 70 ft long and furnished with grave goods, the ship was the last resting place of two women. One suggestion is that they may have been a queen and her daughter. Built slightly later, around 890 CE, and more sturdily than the Oseberg ship, was another Norwegian oak ship, from Gokstad in Vestfold. With a square sail, the 78-foot-long ship could travel at over 12 knots. In 1893, for display at the Chicago World Fair, a full-scale replica crossed the Atlantic from Bergen to New London, Connecticut, in 44 days. Oak was also the main material of the five eleventh-century ships excavated at Skuldelev in Roskilde Fjord, Denmark, in 1962. All were clinker built – with overlapping planks fixed with iron rivets. Of the five, two were stocky cargo ships, one a fishing boat, and two longships. One of the longships was a seagoing warship, some 100 feet long, of oak cut near Dublin, Ireland, dated by its tree rings to around 1042 CE. It could attain a speed of up to 16 knots. Archaeological evidence of Viking shipbuilding skills and the building of replica ships have added substance to the theory that Lief Ericsson (*c.* 970–*c.* 1020 CE) reached North America almost 500 years before Christopher Columbus.

One of the advantages of oak is that some of its branches are naturally crooked: ready grown bowed timber with an unbroken grain along the curve is much stronger than timber sawn to a curve, and simplifies the construction of durable hulls. This is evident in the *Mary Rose*, a warship of some 500 tons, one of the largest ships in the early Tudor navy, built in 1510 primarily of oak. On one estimate, building the *Mary Rose* used the timber of about 600 large oaks that would have occupied 40 acres (16 ha) of woodland scattered over southern England. One of the main deck beams would have weighed nearly three-quarters of a ton. It was an example of England's 'wooden walls'. These both defended the British Isles against Continental neighbours such as the French, Dutch and Spanish and, as larger ships were built, through exploration, trade and colonization, widened the influence of what on the world map was a comparatively small island.

By the end of the Tudor period, in the new Age of Exploration, attention had shifted from royal embroilment in European wars to a wider world of trade and empire building. This is well illustrated in the fortunes of the Smythe family. Thomas 'Customer' Smythe (1522–1591) moved to London at the age of sixteen and later paid the Crown £2,500 to become customs collector for Queen Mary I (r. 1553–8). A rich man, he invested his wealth in ships and their trips, backing explorers of North America such as Sir Walter Raleigh, William Baffin and Sir Humphrey Gilbert. His entrepreneur son, Sir Thomas (1558–1625), at the age of 30, was able to loan Elizabeth I £31,000 to equip ships to sail against the Spanish Armada in 1588. He was the main financier of the Virginia Company's voyage of 1606–7 to Chesapeake Bay to set up England's first successful American colony, Jamestown. In what was to become an empire with a presence in all five continents, initial territories were in North America, India and the Caribbean. The common factor in their discovery and subsequent occupation was ships, oak-bottomed all, extensions of Britain's wooden walls.

Two eighteenth-century examples show the extent and power of 'wooden walls'. Captain James Cook (1728–1779) in HMS *Endeavour* on his first Pacific voyage (1769–71) was nominally on a scientific research expedition with members of the Royal Society, investigating the transit of Venus across the sun and collecting botanical specimens. One of its objectives was finding Terra Australis Incognita, the 'unknown southern land'. Cook also had a mandate to declare British sovereignty over any virgin territory or land, not just small islands, where natives were deemed not to be making use of it. He circumnavigated and charted New Zealand but his greatest prize was in surveying and taking possession of what became New South Wales, the eastern end of what almost amounted to a continent. The size of his achievement is measured against *Endeavour*, a 100-ft (30-m) ship with a white oak hull, copper-sheathed to protect against shipworm, and carrying 94 men and their supplies.

A much bigger ship was HMS *Victory*, launched in 1765. Some 6,000 trees, 90 per cent of them oak, were used in building the 227-ft (70-m) long warship that had a complement of some 850. Its day of glory, 21 October 1805, was under the command of Admiral Horatio Lord Nelson leading the attack on a combined French and Spanish fleet, numbering 33 against the British 27, off southern Spain's Cape

Nelson's flagship, HMS *Victory*, in Portsmouth Historic Dockyard.

Trafalgar. For the British it was the most significant naval battle since Sir Francis Drake's defeat of the Spanish Armada. Outnumbered and outgunned, in three hours the British annihilated the enemy. Napoleon, more successful on land than at sea, immediately abandoned his proposed invasion of Britain. Not until 1940 was there such a comparable victory, this time in the air when fighter aircraft inflicted such damage on the Luftwaffe that Hitler abandoned his intended invasion of Britain.

Patriotic poems and songs from the mid-eighteenth century capture national sentiment. Rule, Britannia (1740) by the Scottish poet James Thomson and set to music by Thomas Arne has the lines:

> Rule, Britannia! rule the waves!
> Britons never will be slaves.

These words in Thomson's original poem are an exhortation and a prediction; within a few years as the song became popular the grammar was altered, changing what was an aim into the insistent, flag-waving 'Britannia rule the waves' and 'Britons never, never, never shall be slaves'. The tone of the lines now expressed a determination and boastful air. This was no doubt the version sung by the crews to bolster their spirits on the eve of Trafalgar. In 1759, a year of victories over the French in British naval history, the actor and playwright David Garrick wrote in his opera *Heart of Oak* the chorus:

> Heart of oak are our ships,
> Heart of oak are our men;
> We are always ready;
> Steady boys, steady;
> We'll fight and we'll conquer again and again.

It became the official march of the Royal Navy, also of the navies of Canada, Australia and New Zealand. In 'Gotham' (1764), the poet Charles Churchill penned the memorable line 'The English Oak, which, dead, commands the flood'. The Scottish poet Thomas Campbell (1777–1844) echoed the thought in *Ye Mariners of England*:

> With thunders from her native oak
> She quells the floods below.

And these stirring words by S. J. Arnold occur as an aria in the opera *The Death of Nelson* (1811):

> Our ships were British oak,
> And hearts of oak our men.

The phrase 'hearts of oak' occurs in the names of a building society, an insurance company, a benefit society, a brand of tobacco and football clubs, including Accra Hearts of Oak, formed in 1911 when Ghana was the Gold Coast colony of the British Empire.

Britain was by no means alone in building ships of oak; competitors were the Netherlands (including the *Amsterdam,* built for trade with the Dutch East Indies); Spain, which had a history of exploration; France, a centralized state that had powers to obtain the best timber in the national interest, whereas Britain had a limited supply from the royal forests and the navy had to deal with contractors; and the USA, which had plentiful supplies of fine-grained white oak. In general, Continental European states such as Austria and Prussia limited colonial aspirations and were more interested in developing armies, which conferred greater social, political and international value. Of greater importance was national outlook. Where was the future of a nation: on land or sea? The question was particularly interesting for Russia. During the fifteenth and sixteenth centuries it had looked north, exploring polar regions. For this it had developed a unique type of ship, a *koch,* a small one- or two-masted ship with rounded lines of the body sitting below the waterline. It also had additional hull planking made of oak or larch that could withstand damage from ice floes.

Hundreds of *koch* were used in the seventeenth-century exploration and conquest of the vast territory of Siberia. Following this, Russia's expansionist policy changed. In 1767 Catherine the Great declared that 'Russia is a European state.' The emphasis was now on large ships such as the twenty-gun brig *Mercury* made of Crimean oak, which had a notable encounter with two Turkish ships in the Russo–Turkish War of 1828–9. This was not the end for the modest *koch.* Its protective features influenced the design of the first modern icebreakers, constructed in the nineteenth century.

Shipbuilding, especially of warships, involved a major investment in time and money. Maintenance was also expensive: wooden bottoms were prone to damage from barnacles, weeds and boring worms such

Ivan Aivazovsky, Brig 'Mercury' Attacked by Two Turkish Ships, 1892, oil on canvas.

as the *Teredo navalis*. An island nation, Britain had no territorial ambitions in Europe, its concern being to maintain a balance of power between Continental nations. Looking outwards to the wider world instead, by the end of the American War of Independence in 1783 it had achieved a naval supremacy lasting well into the nineteenth century. Its enduring legacy was not so much the empire that it enabled, but the export of the English language, an example of a hard wood exerting even more soft power. The Empire is no longer a reality, but English is now spoken by about a quarter of the world's population, the de facto international language of business and technology.

In the days of wooden sailing ships oak was a major resource, but it was only the beginning of a process. Users had to know their wood, what it was capable of, its strengths and weaknesses. The tall load-bearing stern post, for example, had to be a single length of timber without any joints. Phineas Pett (1570–1647), a carpenter who studied ship construction and mathematics and became a shipwright, sometimes hand-selected his own oak. At the time, naval architecture was a relatively new discipline and a learning curve. Stresses and strains had to be understood and plans drawn, performance predicted. When the *Mary Rose* sank in the Solent in 1545, taking with her nearly 700 men, the ambassador of Emperor Charles V reported from Portsmouth that 'When she heeled over with the wind, the water entered by the lowest row of gunports which had been left open after firing.'³ As ship sizes increased and longer voyages were made to farther destinations, other forms and arrangements of sails were tried. Seamanship skills had to be developed and refined: navigation, surveying and map-making.

In England the shipbuilding industry was based near large supplies of oak: the Forest of Dean in the southwest and the New Forest in the south. By the eighteenth century, oak from the Weald of Kent and Sussex was not available in quantity. It was in the south too, especially along the Thames estuary, that the major dockyards were concentrated. Development there spurred growth elsewhere. Sites serving ships had to be updated; new forms of construction had to be devised for lighthouses. Dry docks for ship maintenance date from the seventeenth century. In ports docks too had to be stoutly built.

Greater ships meant there was more at stake. Memories were still strong from one of the greatest maritime disasters in British history, the 1707 sinking of four large ships on rocks off the Isles of Scilly with the loss of nearly 2,000 sailors. That was put down to faulty navigation, a misapprehension of longitude, but granite in the southwest of Britain was a permanent hazard. Not far away in sailing terms were the treacherous Eddystone Rocks off the Devon coast, where a wooden lighthouse had been put into service. It was almost entirely destroyed in the great storm of 1703. A replacement wooden structure around a brick and concrete core lasted from 1709 to 1755. When it burned down the Royal Society recommended John Smeaton (1724–1792), the 'father of civil engineering', to design the third lighthouse. His guiding principle was that, for strength, it should be based on the structure of an oak tree, the deep roots of which anchored it to the ground but allowed it a certain freedom of movement in high winds. The degree of freedom was a risk that could be calculated. Thus the structure, like the rings of a tree, would have a large, heavy base with a curved, tapering pillar above, keeping a low centre of gravity. The exterior consisted of Cornish granite blocks, nearly 1,500 in all, dovetailed with marble dowels and oak pins and secured with quick-drying cement; interior masonry was of Portland stone. The light of the third lighthouse was first lit in 1759; it remained in use until 1877, when the rocks on which it stood had been eroded to the extent that the structure began to shake. Nevertheless, a worldwide standard for lighthouse construction had been established. As a memorial, Smeaton's Tower was dismantled and re-erected on Plymouth Hoe.

The eighteenth century was the period of development of European inland waterways. These were a cheaper means of transport than the inadequate roads and trains of pack animals, especially for bulky goods such as building materials and grain. Where rivers did not meet the need, the answer was man-made canals, sometimes linking rivers to create a transport network, as in Russia.[4] Construction through flat lands was straightforward; on routes with even a slight rise and fall in elevation, boats had to move through locks, often in series. These created a further demand for hard, strong timber. Locks had to withstand the impact of heavily laden barges and boats, and strong gates at each end were needed to contain the volume of water. They were manually operated by massive levers. In frequent use under demanding conditions, the timbers had to last. Towards the end of the twentieth century, British Waterways considered using tropical hardwoods where additional strength or durability was required. A few gates were made with ekki, a dense West African timber significantly heavier than oak, very hard and difficult to machine. Able to withstand tremendous pressures, on some locks it caused problems with the balance and additional load on the pintle. There were further considerations about the environmental impact, the effect on tropical

rainforests and possible carcinogenic dust raised during its preparation. Occasionally greenheart from Guyana is used, but home-grown
oak is the still staple traditional wood.

The construction of inland waterway craft followed the tech-
niques of deep-sea shipbuilding. Inland, wood survived longer than at
sea. Narrowboats were usually built in small yards and docks capable
of working with wood but lacking the capital to invest in the equip-
ment needed for iron and steel fabrication. Wood is also easier to
repair than metal. Thus oak was used for the keelson, which fastened
the keel and the floor timbers together, for the inside timbers and
the hull. The completed craft, perforce of fairly standard dimensions,
was then painted colourfully to give it the individual character that
its owners chose. Oak keelsons were carried over to composite narrow
boat construction, i.e. using wood with iron and steel.[5]

Wood still had its place in steel ships, as on RMS *Titanic*, which
sank after striking an iceberg on its maiden voyage in 1912. What
was once the grand staircase, the first-class entrance aboard, is now
a huge hole in the sunken wreck. There were two such staircases,
one fore, one aft. The oak-panelled fore descended five levels from
the boat deck to E deck, its clock surrounded by an intricate oak
carving depicting Honour and Glory crowning Time. Microbes have
now eaten away the wood. The aft staircase was torn apart as the
Titanic broke up shortly before sinking. All is not lost, however. Ban-
isters from the grand staircase of the *Titanic*'s sister ship the *Olympic*
are preserved in the White Swan Hotel in Alnwick, Northumber-
land, where the dining room is lined with panelling from her
first-class lounge.

Oak did not entirely cease to be the main material for seagoing
craft. The first America's Cup, the international yachting trophy, was
won in 1851 by *America,* a 100-ft (30-m) schooner with an oak hull.
It was built for a New York investor for $30,000 on a no-win-no-
fee basis. *Bluenose*, taking its name from the eighteenth-century
nickname for Nova Scotians, was both a racing ship and a working
fishing schooner. Built at Lunenberg in 1921, its frames, timbers, rails

and deck furniture were of oak. Its primary purpose was fishing in the Grand Banks off the Newfoundland coast, which it did until the end of the Second World War. As a bonus, beating off American and Canadian competition, for eighteen years it held the International Fishermen's Trophy for speed.

Naval architecture continued to have an influence back on land. George Bernard Shaw's play *Heartbreak House* (1919) is set in

> a room which has been built so as to resemble the after-part of an old-fashioned high-pooped ship with a stern gallery; for the windows are ship built with heavy timbering . . .

Portcullis House, the Westminster office building opened in 2001 for Members of Parliament and their staff, was designed to look and feel like a ship inside. All the offices and passages are made with bowed windows and light oak finishes.

Various means of terrestrial transport had long relied upon a basis in oak. Trackways and causeways to dry land had thick foundations of tree trunks, sometimes laid at right angles, packed with loose twigs and surmounted by brushwood. A similar method of construction was used for the creation of prehistoric artificial islands, lake dwellings or Gaelic crannogs. In swamps, marshes and peat bogs these platforms, prone to sinking, had to be renewed periodically to afford safe passage and a safe home. As many as fourteen superimpositions have been recorded, which points to continuous occupation, perhaps as long as 150 years, and suggests that the work involved co-operative effort. Stout oak timbers were also used for piles around the edges of huts and palisades for defence of a settlement. The idea may well have originated in Alpine areas, such sites from the Late Bronze Age and Iron Age having been discovered in northern Italy and southern Germany. Outside the lake village at Glastonbury, Somerset, an oak door 3.5 ft x 1.5 ft, probably half of a double swing door, was discovered in the peat.

The Romans made an even greater use of oak piles, such as in the piles for the bridge across the River Medway on the route from the Channel port of Dover to London. For each of the nine piers, a coffer-dam was created from a double ring of piles. Oak piles tipped with iron were driven into the chalk bedrock and on this foundation a timber framework was erected, surrounded with stone masonry and the centre filled with ragstone rubble to form a pier. On top of the timber roadway three oak beams were laid between each pier and then the planks forming the road surface. Similarly, the original London Bridge was built in around 55 CE to take the place of the pontoon bridge to the north bank of the Thames that the Romans had laid down about five years earlier. Oaks some 300 years old were felled in the Thames Valley and floated down the river. They have been perfectly preserved in the waterlogged ground, as have the remnants of quays and rectangular timber-framed buildings. Together, they add up to an impression of what life was like in the future capital at the time: 'That early London the Romans built must have had the timber-clad look and bustle of a Wild West boom town.'[6] Later, from 240–360 CE, when the riverside wall of the city completed the defence of Londinium, timber foundations supported the stone. Early on in the Roman occupation, oak piles were also used in the public baths at Bath spa. The Romans built to last and, along with many of their buildings, their principles survived. As early as the eleventh century, the northern Russian city of Novgorod, which along with its cathedral St Sophia, modelled on the building of the same name in Constantinople, had streets paved with oak beams and oak drains and gutters. Founded in the late twelfth century, the Dutch city of Amsterdam was based on oak piles supplemented by alder, fir and poplar. Constructed at the end of the nineteenth century, Hamburg Rathaus (city hall) stands on 4,000 oak piles.

When a wheel turns, each spoke in turn takes the weight that the wheel is carrying. Hence it is important that a wooden wheel is constructed of properly seasoned timbers that have been air-dried for as long as five years. Spokes were usually made of heart of the oak, the strongest part with the straightest grain and without knots. A spoke was fashioned with a spokeshave while the hub or nave, usually of elm but sometimes oak, was turned on a lathe. Mortises took the ends of the spokes. Hence a wheelwright, a tradesman found in most villages, was a skilled craftsman. His vanished craft is described by George Sturt in *The Wheelwright's Shop* (1923). In motion, early wheels turned on the fixed axle, causing friction and wear. From the evidence of a first-century BCE funeral wagon discovered in Denmark, a solution seems to date from the Iron Age. An extension of the oak hub was lined on the inside with semicircular grooves each containing a small hardwood roller. These bearings rotated as the wheel turned, thus rolling on the axle instead of scraping around it. Friction was thus reduced.[7] Oak was also used for the axle bed and in the main frame of farm carts and wagons designed to carry heavy loads. Covered wagons, also known as prairie schooners, were made of hickory, oak or maple that would endure the long, rough journeys of the pioneers crossing the U.S. in the nineteenth century.

Although there had been a considerable increase in the application of iron and steel in the nineteenth century, wood was still used when the first motorized vehicles were built. For instance, the English and German Dogcarts, first manufactured in 1895, on which the driver and passenger sat in the open air, had an oak or ash frame. The larger rear wheels where made of oak, as were wheels in the many designs of what became the bicycle. Some velocipedes had oak frames, hubs, spokes and handlebar. In 1877, an American inventor, George Sheffield, who had a 7-mile walk to work, devised a velocipede to operate on a railroad track. Two wheels fitted on one side of the track and, joined by oak struts, a balancing third wheel sat on the opposite rail. It was a forerunner of the railroad handcar on which maintenance workers pumped their way along. In Europe from the Middle Ages to the late eighteenth century, rails themselves had been made of oak, the same heavy-duty material used for the trucks carrying ores and coal from quarries and mines; while oak treenails fastened rails to sleepers.

For mines, pit props were produced from relatively short, straight lengths of coppiced timber. Similar timber was needed by the iron and glass industries, charcoal being produced as the fuel for smelting ore. Timber too good to burn could harness the power of nature, water and wind. Waterwheels needed heavy framework and drive shafts at least were commonly of oak. The Romans employed vertical wheels, operated by treadwheels, as a means of raising water from mines, in deep mines arranging wheels in a sequence to a point where the water could be drained away. Another way of using water power was to operate a trip hammer that broke ore-bearing rock.[8] Oak was much used in the twelfth-century tide mill discovered at Greenwich, which drew water from the Thames when it rose and released it as the tide ebbed, grinding corn into flour. An oak trough to channel the water was shaped out of a single oak beam; oak piles anchored the superstructure on the wet ground at the edge of the river. The wheel was large, over five metres in diameter. Large too, perhaps as much as 40 ft (12 m) long and 2 ft^2 (0.6 m) at the ends, was the central post about which a post windmill rotated to face into the wind. Behind the sails was the oak head wheel with its precisely cut, bevelled teeth, often nearly a hundred of them. A head wheel was also part of a smock mill, one in which the body of the mill does not move, only the cap. In both types of mill engineering, parts such as gears were either of oak or elm to withstand wear. The same was true of pulleys for lifting heavy loads.

Oak retained its role in the manufacture of engineering parts into the Industrial Revolution. For smoother operation and longer life, large gears and brake wheels were often meshed with other close-grained hardwoods such as apple, beech, holly and hornbeam. Similar combinations were made in the construction of simple tumbler locks. The prize for precision must go to clock manufacture, specifically to John Harrison (1693–1776). The son of a carpenter, he followed his father in that trade, building and repairing clocks in his spare time.

In 1713 he built his first longcase clock, in which the mechanism was made entirely of wood. In the early 1720s Harrison was commissioned to make a new turret clock for the stable block at Brocklesby Park in north Lincolnshire. The principle was again of meshing to reduce friction. Oak-toothed wheels meshed with components – rollers, bushes and discs – of lignum vitae, a tropical hardwood that has the useful property of being self-lubricating. Hence a clock using it does not need oiling, which not only saves labour but also makes for greater accuracy as the viscosity of oil varies with temperature. The oak Harrison used was not of one quality: the wheel teeth were from fast-growing trees with a wide grain and great strength; the centre of the wheels was of lighter weight wood from a slow-growing tree. Harrison's design and manufacture have stood the test of time; apart from a brief planned refurbishment in 1884, the clock has been running continuously. He went on to make three precision pendulum clocks based on the same principle, and later designed an accurate portable watch that Captain Cook took on his second voyage. However, Harrison's greatest achievement was the invention of the marine chronometer, which enabled mariners to establish their longitude at sea, with a consequent increase in safe navigation.

In the U.S. Eli Terry (1772–1852), a Connecticut clockmaker, heavily influenced by the ideas of another Connecticut manufacturer, Eli Whitney (1765–1825), inventor of the cotton gin, was instrumental in revolutionizing clock production. Whitney advocated four advances: the use of power machinery; interchangeable parts; the division of labour; and the creation of an assembly line. Terry began making clocks when at the time the choice was between brass and wooden components. Brass was comparatively expensive, difficult to work with and labour-intensive. Hence clocks were costly and were peddled individually in a limited market. At first Terry divided the labour among apprentices who, whittling with a pocketknife, rough cut the wooden wheels. Their work was then handed on to skilled and higher paid journeymen, who worked precisely. Terry's next step was to replace the apprentices with water power. In 1807, when a skilled craftsman

Some of the moving parts of John Harrison's famous clocks were
made out of dense and durable oak.

could turn out six to ten clocks a year, he took the bold step of sign-
ing a contract to produce 4,000 clocks in four years. The first two
years were mainly spent on developing the system. In the third year
he fulfilled the order. He had made the transition from craftsman to
mass manufacturer, producing more affordable clocks, but it was
Henry Ford who was to receive the recognition for creating a mass
market for a consumer product.

Mechanization of wider significance was speeding up the production of thread in the textile industry, a major advance since the
Middle Ages and an early step in the Industrial Revolution that was
to have profound effects on society at large. Apprenticed to a barber
and wigmaker, Richard Arkwright (1732–1792) had a feeling for the
behaviour of natural fibres and an aptitude for practical mechanics.
Thus he understood the kind of pressures that would have to be
exerted on cotton fibres if they were going to be turned into thread.
Where others had failed, he eventually succeeded in inventing a
spinning machine, his first model being made entirely of oak and

patented in 1769. It consisted of four rollers rotating in sequence at increasing speeds to draw out the fibres, which were then fed to a flyer that twisted them and wound the thread on to a bobbin. Power for his vertical spinning mill was supplied by a waterwheel and his invention was known as a 'water frame'. Each advance in processes, say in spinning and weaving, drew attention to lagging technologies holding up textile productivity. Other entrepreneurs were encouraged to engage in profitable catch-up, mechanizing every stage of the process. As a result, skilled crafts exercised in cottage industry gave way to mass production in the factory system; the cotton industry grew at the expense of the wool; more goods were produced at lower cost; exports prospered.

Skills in cleaving round timber for making farm tools, baskets, posts, fencing, gates and ladders survived longer in the countryside. There was nothing new about ladders; a long one dating from the mid-first century CE was found in the excavations of Roman London. There was not much rural opposition to change; traditional methods had their advantages. For example, cleaving with simple tools instead of sawing keeps to the natural grain of the wood, retaining its tough, durable quality.

Other crafts demonstrated the skill of the man who knew his materials and his trade. In his *Lives*, Plutarch (*c. 46–c. 120 CE*) remarked that 'Aegeus gave a scarlet sail dyed with the juice of the flower of a very flourishing holm-oak.'[9] Tannin (the word is derived from *tanna*, Old High German for oak) has industrial applications. The chemical is produced by the oak marble gall, a growth caused by a type of gall wasp, which lays its eggs within the leaf buds and is responsible for most of the galls that develop on an oak. Galls form, supplying the insect larvae with food and protecting them from predators and the weather. Marble galls contain high levels of tannic acid, which can be extracted by soaking the bark, which should be stripped in springtime from newly felled oaks. It has the useful property of halting the natural decay of animal hides and skins and turning them into leather that is both tough and supple. Leather use is subject to fashion. From 1780 to 1850 there was a boom in the use of leather in the UK. The industry was a bigger consumer of oak trees than the naval dockyards, and almost certainly than the merchant shipyards. Thousands of acres were maintained as oak underwood, in which timber production was sacrificed for a greater yield of bark.[10] Moreover, leather can be dyed, as can cloth, using tannin; the process was known even in ancient China. The dye was also used cosmetically, and Nicholas Culpeper's *The English Physician* (1652) mentions oak galls being used for dyeing hair black.

Similar to dyeing is the manufacture of oak ink, which is remarkably durable, enabling scholars to read and others to examine today manuscripts penned by monks in the Dark Ages, such as the seventh-century gospel of St Cuthbert. Tannin produces a dark or black ink. Addition of a binder such as gum arabic, exuded by certain species of acacia, held the ink firmly to vellum or parchment. Thus natural products result in manuscripts durable for centuries. Resistant to rubbing or washing, they retain their fresh appearance. A few centuries earlier the wood was used as a recording material. The Romans created not only physical communications in the form of ports, roads, bridges

Wooden writing tablets from the Roman fort of Vindolanda on Hadrian's Wall.

and signal towers but also person-to-person literate links, as ancient wooden tablets found at Vindolanda, a fort and civilian settlement just south of Hadrian's Wall, shows. Roman writing is usually associated with wax tablets, but the Vindolanda tablets are made of thin wood, local alder, birch and oak no more than 3 mm thick. Hundreds have survived in the damp underground of Roman rubbish pits.

Acorns that have high starch content are a source of methanol, more commonly known as 'wood alcohol'. Oak has been used in wine making since the Roman Republic. Even in modern wineries where production involves the use of stainless steel tanks, oak chips contained in fabric bags assume some of the role of the conventional barrel. There is no substitute, though, for the real thing and the specialist skill of the cooper, rooted in rural tradition. Having served a long apprenticeship in making barrels and casks, the cooper first has to select his high-quality seasoned oak. Natural seasoning is a slow process; kiln drying is faster but doesn't soften tannin in wine as much.

Extracting juice from grapes in a wooden wine press, or oil from seeds such as rape or sesame, is a short process, whereas it takes anything from months to years to mature beer, wine and distilled spirits. However much is known about the chemistry of the process, art and experience have to be brought to bear. Sherry and whisky, for instance, have a unique taste only developed in oak casks, dense white oak being ideal. Cognac does well in casks of oak from the Limousin forest in south-central France, the loosely grained wood making the oak flavour more pronounced. Woods have to be matched to intended contents. Poorly chosen wood can adversely affect the taste of a brand, disappointing loyal drinkers and impairing the investment. Hence the importance of established, trusting relationships between wood suppliers and wineries in countries with a large wine and spirits industry. Before the Russian Revolution of 1917, oak from the Baltic states was frequently used by French winemakers. Today Russian oak from the Adygey along the Black Sea is being explored by winemakers as

However much modern machinery is used in oak barrel manufacture, the traditional craftsman's skills are still needed.

a cheaper alternative to home-grown oak. In France, a major source of oak for storing cognacs and *grands vins*, especially of Burgundy, is the central Forêt de Tronçais. According to the Scotch Whisky Association, financing maturing stocks is the most significant capital investment the industry has to make. Furthermore, the cask must not only be absolutely watertight but also retain the volatile spirits that could evaporate over the years. The porous nature of oak allows a degree of oxygenation and evaporation, the 'angels' share', but it has to be within limits. Hence only well-seasoned oak can be used and it must be knot-free. The cooper first cleaves it into staves, then hollows the inner surface, bevels the edges, cuts grooves at top and bottom, forces temporary hoops over the staves to bring the bevels together in a perfect joint, lights a small fire in the cask to heat the wood and make it more flexible, fits the ends of the cask, caulks it, and finally fits permanent hoops. Before use the cask is tested for watertightness.

New barrels release more flavour than previously used barrels. Often barrels are reused, sometimes rebuilt with a mixture of old and new staves to achieve the amount of tannin desired for a particular

Cork oaks with stripped bark in southern Spain.

product. Having served in a winery for a few years, during which time any flavour of the oak barrel has leached out, barrels may well be reused in a Canadian, European or Japanese distillery. U.S. laws state that whisky has to be aged in new oak barrels, so there is a thriving international trade in previously used barrels from Kentucky. The makers of Jim Beam bourbon whisky point out that in new charred oak barrels the charring caramelizes sugars in the wood. This reaction of the wood trying to heal itself from the heat adds to the flavour of the bourbon.

The rate of maturation depends on various factors: the size of the cask; where the casks are stored; and temperature and humidity changes within the store. Tasters check small samples to determine when the spirit is ready for bottling. Here again oak has a role, corks coming from the cork oak. Its thick layer of lightweight bark can be harvested at eight to ten year intervals without permanent damage to the tree, as it renews itself.

Shipping wine in barrels has not always been best for the product, particularly when done slowly in excessive heat. All the careful work of raising the grapes and producing a vintage could be spoilt in transit, ending in what the French called *vinaigre*, literally 'sour wine'. To salvage what might have been a total loss, a by-product was created, vinegar. A medieval centre of this was the port of Orléans, where an industry grew along the wharves of the river Loire handling spoiled barrels

Shipping wine in oak barrels in France.

of wines. The traditional method has been continued and made a virtue of. For example, fresh tarragon is fermented for at least six months with white wine from the Loire Valley in partially filled oak barrels, some of the mixture being old wine. It is marketed as wine or gourmet vinegar, a superior salad dressing. Italian balsamic vinegar is aged in oak barrels for longer periods.

At War

In military applications, the timber has been used both for defence and attack: in defence in the form of palisades and in attack as various weapons. Frequently used in the Hundred Years War (1337–1453) between England and France was the longbow, made of yew, later of ash or elm, with arrows of oak, ash or elm. Oak was used to test fire-power, and modern experiments have shown that medieval claims were not exaggerated. From 200 metres a long bow could penetrate over an inch of solid oak, equivalent to the density of armour of the time. Plate armour could be penetrated at a range of 100 metres.

Made of over 300 pieces of oak was the trebuchet, a medieval siege engine for hurling projectiles at enemy walls. Qualities such as strength, weight and resistance to splintering were integral in making a weapon in which the owner would have confidence. Shafts of javelins and pikes could be of oak. A shillelagh, taking its eighteenth-century name from a barony and village in County Wicklow, is an Irish cudgel of black-thorn or oak.

It is in Japan that the widest use has been made of individual weapons. During the Muromachi period (1392–1568) the style of combat changed, from fighting on a battlefield to duelling with a single opponent. The heroes of Japan's feudal society were its samu-rai, whose power was to last until the Meiji Restoration in 1868. Male and female warriors already used the *naginata*, a weapon similar to the pike in having a wooden shaft but with a curved blade at the end. Constructed from natural materials, say white oak for the shaft and bamboo for a cutting edge, with its long range it was effective in

As part of its re-creation of 14th-century life, including siege engines, the Danish Medieval Centre has reconstructed this counterweight trebuchet.

conflict with mounted knights and cheaper to make than highly prized swords. Growing use of firearms in the seventeenth century and the abolition of the samurai after 1868 meant that martial arts came to be used more for self-defence and as competitive sports, with emphasis on the disciplines benefiting the body and mind. The *bokken* is a solid white oak training tool for using a traditional Japanese sword.

A *jo*, a staff made in various lengths and weights, was in combat a match for a sword; it is still used today by some Japanese police forces.

As with other commodities, demand for wood fluctuates with changes in fashion and technologies. In the past oak has been one of the preferred hardwoods for coffin construction. Today there are cheaper alternatives used in cremations, notably cardboard, decorated if desired, and chipboard, tastefully disguised. Metals have taken the place of wood in the construction of ships and the manufacture of many industrial products. Against this, in developed countries there is something of a return to traditional crafts and materials. There should always be a demand for one of nature's most useful woods. Its essential qualities have not changed.

five

Wood in Words

❦

Having so many uses at various times in different places, the oak has given rise to many sayings. As the American novelist William Faulkner (1897–1962) wrote, 'Words are like acorns . . . Every one of 'em won't make a tree, but if you just have enough of 'em, you're bound to get a tree.'

Of the attributes of the tree, the quality most dwelled upon is its nobility. In *The Task* (1785) the poet William Cowper called it 'Lord of the woods, the long-surviving oak'.[1] In *Woodlands* (1859) W. S. Coleman wrote of 'The majestic oak, the Monarch of the forest'.[2] To the poet laureate Alfred, Lord Tennyson (1809–92) in one of his later poems, 'The Oak', it was an example to be followed:

> Live thy Life,
> Young and old,
> Like yon oak,
> Bright in spring,
> Living gold;
>
> Summer-rich,
> Then; and then
> Autumn-changed
> Soberer-hued
> Gold again.

> All his leaves
> Fall'n at length,
> Look, he stands,
> Trunk and bough,
> Naked strength.

Also associating the tree with tenacity, a French proverb: 'A woman on her back is as strong as an upright oak' (*La femme sur son dos est aussi fort qu'un chêne debout*). Even in pathetic fallacy, words of nobility ring true, as in *Hyperion*, John Keats's abandoned epic fragment drafted in the winter and spring of 1818–19:

> As when, upon a trancèd summer-night,
> Those green-robed senators of mighty woods,
> Tall oaks, branch-charmèd by the earnest stars,
> Dream, and so dream all night without a stir . . .[3]

The phrase 'hearts of oak' is thought by the British to be a quintessentially British one, embodying all that goes with the virtue of unyielding strength. The concept is in fact much older; a hardened heart occurs in the two great classical epics. Early in Book XII of the *Odyssey*, the enchantress Circe welcomes Odysseus after his return from the underworld with the lines:

> Hearts of oak, did you go down
> Alive into the homes of death? One visit
> Finishes all men but yourselves, twice mortal![4]

In Book IV of *The Aeneid*, citing divine command, Aeneas justifies his departure to Dido, suffering the pangs of unrequited love:

> She had spoken. He set his gaze firmly on Jupiter's
> warnings, and hid his pain steadfastly in his heart.[5]

An 'oaken heart' sounds more obdurate than a hard heart, just as 'oaken men' seem tougher than mere strong men. According to the playwright William Congreve (1670–1729) in his only tragedy, *The Mourning Bride*, this heart could, however, be moved:

> Music hath charms to soothe a savage breast
> To soften rocks, or bend a knotted oak.

Hearts of Oak was the name of two eighteenth-century protest movements. In Ireland it was the name of a non-sectarian secret society, also called the Oak Boys or Green Boys, flourished briefly from 1763, when it conducted a campaign against landlords raising rents and exacting tithes. Just before the outbreak of the American War of Independence, a volunteer militia including students, among them the future leader of the Federalist Party, Alexander Hamilton (1757–1804), was formed in New York City. These 'hearts of oak' wore a badge of red tin hearts with the words 'God and our Right' on their green tunics. *Hearts of Oak* (1924) was also a 50-minute silent drama directed by John Ford, but we do not know its content because the film is believed to be lost.

Other sayings are specific to a particular place and period. In the Czech Republic the meaning of proverb 'When the oak leaves fall' is brought out in the modern fairy tale, by Jan Werich, *Fimfarum* (1960):

> A farmer's wife demanded that her husband decide what he wanted more, her or the demon drink. Unable to make up his mind, he went for a walk. A storm arose and suddenly he was confronted by a hairy devil, who said 'I'll help you with your problem in return for your signing your soul to me in blood'. Their Faustian pact was agreed. The farmer returned to his wife, who later bore him a son. As time went by the farmer became increasingly uneasy, fearing what he had done. This came to a head when one summer day he saw a curt note in an apple tree 'Next week'. Scared, he got drunk. Fortunately, he

met an old lady, who advised him that he should only go 'when the oak leaves fall, which they never do because the wise old oak never sheds all its leaves'. Is it because the oak has the power to protect people or is it just a proverb? Either way, like tomorrow, 'when the oak leaves fall' never comes.

The proverb is akin to the French *payer en feuilles de chêne, payer en effets sans valeur* (paying in oak leaves means paying in worthless currency).

In slang, the oak has over time acquired more respectable associations. In late Tudor and early Stuart times an 'oak' was one who in a highway robbery kept a lookout on behalf of the highwayman. It also applied to a team of confidence tricksters. But from the late seventeenth to the mid-nineteenth centuries 'oak' was shorthand for a person of good standing, somebody to be relied upon. It also had a role in maintaining law and order: an 'oaken towel' was a cudgel or policeman's club. Thus to 'rub somebody down with an oaken towel' was to give him a beating, for short a 'towelling'. The sporting novelist R. S. Surtees (1805–1864) captured the threat of punishment in *Handley Cross* (1843):

> If you persist in playin' at marbles, chuck farthin', and flyin' kites, instead of attendin' in the stable, I'll send you back to the charity school from whence you came, where you'll be rubbed down twice a day with an oak towel.[6]

'Felling of oaks' is a now-obsolete term for seasickness that may have had its origin in vomiting aboard an oak-planked ship. An oak can mean a stupid person whereas an 'oak tree' is a big, tall, strong, young male.

In rhyming slang an 'oak' is a joke and 'oak and ash' is cash. A contrary meaning is contained in 'coals and coke' or Hearts of Oak: broke, as in this piece of Cockney rhyming slang:

Gorblimey, I got a wife an' Gord-forbids [kids] at 'ome; so I takes a chance an' stands for a minute by Tottenham Court Road Station. An' up come a bleedn' rozzer [policeman] an' lumbers me. Wot a life! Coppers! That's wot we pays 'em for – to take the bleedn' strike-me-dead [bread] out of yer children's mouf. Forty bob or a month. It left me 'earts-of-oak.[7]

In the U.S. an 'oakley', so called after the performer Annie Oakley, who achieved a second bout of fame with Irving Berlin's musical *Annie Get Your Gun* (1946), was a free pass, originally to a circus and later to a theatre. An 'oakey' is a white person way down the social scale, second only to trailer trash, but by contrast, an outstanding individual is summed up in the acronym OAK, 'One of A Kind'. In the knowledge economy the acronym occurs in various forms: Open Access to Knowledge; Opportunities And Knowledge; Older Adult Knowledge. Oak was the original name for a programming language written in 1991 by James Gosling, a Canadian working for Sun Microsystems; he named the language after a tree standing outside his office in Silicon Valley. Because of a likely confusion with the products of Oak Technology, a maker of semiconductor chips, the name of the enhanced language was changed in 1994 to Java. Oak also forms part of the name for a number of software packages. There are many more uses of the word, often scatological and temporary, and local shorthand (e.g. for Oakland Raiders, a professional football team).

Proverbs on the topic tend to focus on optimism and patience, emphasizing potential and growth. A German folk tale relates the ruse of a farmer outwitting the Devil, to whom he had promised his soul, by securing a reprieve until his first crop was harvested. The farmer planted acorns, and waited . . . In one of the Icelandic epics, *Egil's Saga* (c. 1240), a character refers to an old saw 'He must tend the oak who is to dwell beneath it'.[8] An often-quoted example is the observation that 'every oak has been an acorn'. On the other hand, 'The acorn becomes an oak by means of automatic growth. No commitment is necessary.' 'Great oaks from little acorns grow' and 'Today's mighty oak is yesterday's little nut that held its ground' are variations on the call for patience in the young in 'Lines written for a School Declamation' by David Everett (1770–1813):

> Large streams from little fountains flow,
> Tall oaks from little acorns grow.

Other proverbs have similar themes: 'Storms make oaks take deeper roots' and 'Oaks grow strong in contrary winds and diamonds are made under pressure' are but two. Another:

> Many a genius has been slow of growth. Oaks that flourish
> for a thousand years do not spring into beauty like a reed.

The preacher Henry Ward Beecher (1813–1887) contradicted this however, when he stated that 'Genius unexerted is no more genius than a bushel of acorns is a forest of oaks.' And according to the Chinese sage Confucius (551–479 BCE): 'The green reed which bends in the wind is stronger than the mighty oak which breaks in a storm.' Pick your oak proverb or observation according to the point you want to make. Comparisons with other trees can teach a lesson: 'The willow will buy a horse before the oak will pay for a saddle', and Edward H. Richards makes the point:

> A wise old owl sat on an oak;
> The more he saw the less he spoke;
> The less he spoke the more he heard;
> Why aren't we like that wise old bird?

Longevity is at the mercy of repeated attacks: 'An oak is not felled at one stroke' and 'Little strokes fell great oaks', or, as John Lyly (*c.* 1554–1606) put it in his prose romance *Euphues: The Anatomy of Wit* (1579), 'Many strokes overthrow the tallest oaks'. The death of an oak has to be seen in perspective, as Thomas Carlyle (1795–1881) pointed out in his essay *On History*: 'When the oak-tree is felled, the whole forest echoes with it; but a hundred acorns are planted silently by some unnoticed breeze.' Erasmus Darwin (1731–1802), grandfather of the naturalist Charles Darwin, regarded nature as even more generous in ensuring the survival of a species, writing:

> Each pregnant Oak ten thousand acorns forms
> Profusely scattered by autumnal storms.[9]

To 'sport the oak' was a term common in British universities in the nineteenth and twentieth centuries, the 'oak' being an outer door to a room. To close this was an indication that the occupant of the room was busy, possibly even doing some work. Its purpose is made clear to an Oxford first-year in *The Adventures of Mr Verdant Green* by Cuthbert Bede, the pen name of the humorous writer Edward Bradley (1827–1889):

> Mr Filcher, a scout [a male college servant], then went on to point out the properties of the rooms, and also their mechanical contrivances.
> 'This is the hoak [oak], this 'ere outer door is, sir, where the gentlemen sports, that is to say, shuts, sir, when they're a readin'. Not as Mr Smalls ever hinterfered with his constitootion by too much 'ard study, sir; he only sported his hoak when people used to get troublesome about their little bills.'[10]

The oak tree has a historical role as a weather forecaster. Simple indications are taken as a guide to the weather outlook. In Spain, farmers examine oak galls to check when wheat is ready for harvest. If there is a maggot within, the yield should be good; if the insect has already hatched, the opposite is true. The oak being one of the last trees to shed its leaves is the basis of the couplet

> If on the trees the leaves still hold,
> The coming winter will be cold.

Dating from the eighteenth century, and its place of origin claimed among others as Ireland and Lincolnshire, is the rhyme

> If the oak's before the ash,
> Then we'll only have a splash;
> If the ash before the oak, then we'll surely have a soak.

The timing refers to the appearance of the first buds and their leaves. If the oak is first, the summer will be dry; if the ash is first, then it will be a wet summer. This has some scientific basis: the ash has shallower roots than the oak, which means that the oak fares better in drier conditions. This is being accentuated by climate change. Global warming favours the oak, the leaves of which can gain a bigger share of summer sunlight and use up more water. Dr Kate Lewthwaite of the Woodland Trust explains:

> With every one degree rise in temperature, oak has a four-day advantage over ash. Ash appears to be more responsive to the length of the day in spring, while oak is more responsive to temperature. So, with warmer springs, oak is having the advantage.[11]

In a Darwinian struggle for competitive advantage, the face of the forest is changing. Dominance of oak over ash has consequences for wildlife too, altering the familiar timetable for the hundreds of insects for which it is a food source. Another rhyme linking the two trees warns of the danger in sheltering under a tree during a thunderstorm:

> Beware the oak it draws a stroke,
> Avoid an ash it counts the flash.

There is a physical basis for the saying in that the oak, large in the landscape, has a low electrical resistance. Hence the blasted oak, stark in silhouette and with a haunting character.

However, this did not stop the wood being the choice for the solid construction of the electric chair, the first of which was used in New York State in 1890. A strong chair was necessary to withstand the effects of the 2,250 volt charges, each normally of three seconds in length, repeated four times within two minutes, sent through the body of the occupant restrained by leather straps. One nickname for the chair was 'Thunderbolt'. There was a particularly gruesome practice in Florida, where inmates of the state prison made their 'Old Sparky' in 1923 after the state legislature designated electrocution the official method of execution in place of hanging. A three-legged replacement was constructed from oak in 1998. Out on a heath in a storm, King Lear cries:

'Old Sparky' was used in over 100 executions between 1926 and 1948 in a unit of the Arkansas Department of Correction.

You sulphurous and thought-executing fires,
Vaunt couriers of oak-cleaving thunderbolts,
Singe my white head![12]

In some myths the oak tree is actually sacred to the gods of thunder and lightning.

six

Symbols and Superstitions

ᒼᕉᓭ

A s well as the basic necessities of life – food, clothing and shelter – early man wanted security. Not just physical protection from enemies but more important, the psychological security of knowing. He needed to know where he stood in the scheme of things, what lay ahead in an uncertain world where life was short and living could be precarious. Would he be fortunate in hunting for meat and gathering fruits? What would the weather be for growing and harvest, and next winter? Were there malign forces to be propitiated?

In this deep quandary, the oak offered some reassurance, some hope for prehistoric man. The tree started life as one of many seeds that could have been eaten by animals and birds. Somehow the fortunate acorns grew and survived to lead a long life. Of all the trees in the forest it was the most enduring and solid wood, hard to work, but worth the effort. An inspiration, it was a worthy material for creating a place of worship or celebration. Evidence survives that confirms it was used in building sacred or significant sites. Further sites may yet be discovered. It is reasonable to regard these man-made structures as major centres, the temples of their time: more numerous would have been lesser shrines; oak groves, their status completely lost. We can imagine the virtues of the oak being discussed by the elders in a community, stories being told and beliefs being reinforced. Over time and through this process, the attributes and features of this tree accumulated a wealth of symbolism and superstitions.

The acorn, in Greek *balanos*, in Latin *glans*, was a symbol of reproduction. In its cup it was just like the tip of the penis, the *glans penis*. This association is made in a feature of the paintings of nude youths in the Sistine Chapel by Michelangelo (1475–1564). Most of the twenty young men, more classical than Christian, wear a garland of oak leaves. Around them are clusters of acorns looking more like the glans penis than acorns. They are an in-joke with his patron, Pope Julius II (1503–1513), who like his uncle Pope Sixtus IV, who was responsible for building the Sistine Chapel, had the family name della Rovere ('of the oak tree'), and perhaps also a reflection of Michelangelo's sexual orientation.

From the penis came semen, not unlike the milky liquid in mistletoe berries. Kissing under the mistletoe has endured as a custom. Whether or not a lover would marry could be divined by dropping two acorns, one for each of the couple, into a basin of water. Floating close together indicated a wedding, whilst apart indicated no such

This nude figure by Michelangelo in the ceiling of the Sistine Chapel, Rome, carries an oak and acorn cornucopia.

A phallic Danish
oak figurine of
c. 600 BC, found in
Broddenbjerg bog
near Viborg.

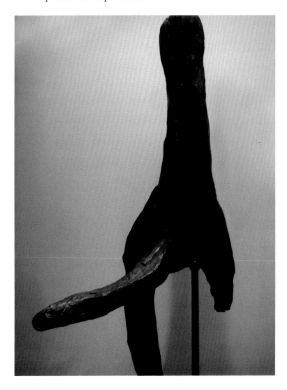

luck. Such a wedding might take place beneath a sacred tree, a marriage oak, around which the couple would dance and perhaps carve a cross as a permanent reminder of the occasion. A May fertility rite was cutting green oak boughs for decorating house doorways; at the same time, in what was a semi-pagan ritual, a marriage bough was hauled up the outside of the local church tower and hung out to bless newly married couples. The tree itself might be seen as a phallic symbol, a notion surviving in the maypole. So many early beliefs and practices are but a shadow of themselves in sanitized ceremonies still held today, their participants and spectators unaware of their origins and significance. The origin of some local customs, for instance feasting on the top of an oak, is a matter of conjecture.

Said to be the most ancient oracle of the Greeks, Dodona, a sanctuary of Zeus, was centred around a sacred oak tree. Individuals and representatives of states came to Epirus in northwest Greece to consult it. Messages came in the form of whisperings from or markings on the oak's leaves, which were interpreted by priestesses. Athena, daughter of Zeus and the goddess of intellect, had a branch of the speaking oak set in the prow of the *Argo,* the ship the hero Jason and the Argonauts sailed to retrieve the Golden Fleece, itself suspended from an ancient oak and guarded by a monstrous serpent. A mythological radar, the wood enabled the *Argo* to receive warnings of dangers ahead.

Zeus' Roman equivalent, Jupiter, had a grove of sacred trees surrounding the hilltop temple dedicated to him at Cumae, near Naples. Here the most famous of the sibyl prophets wrote her prophesies on oak leaves, which were arranged inside the entrance to her cave. If disturbed by the wind, the Cumaean Sibyl would not put them back into order.

Dryads, the attendants of the goddess Artemis (Diana in Roman mythology), were the nymphs of oak trees; later the term covered trees in general. Any mortal who harmed trees without first propitiating the tree nymphs was punished by the gods. That was the fate of Erysichthon who, in need of timber, started cutting down a sacred grove belonging to Demeter, a goddess of fertility. He ignored the goddess's warning against felling a giant oak that stood in the grove and which was home to a dryad nymph, and was cursed to suffer insatiable hunger, which ruined him and his household. Zeus, whose name is related to the word 'sky', was the most powerful of the Greek gods, the authority on everything human and divine. As the sky god, he kept a fatherly eye on the world and was responsible for communications between heaven and earth. No wonder that on the orders of the Roman emperor Theodosius I (347–395 CE), a Christian who conducted an anti-pagan crusade, the oak at Dodona was destroyed in the year 391. Modern archaeologists have planted a new oak on the site.

DRYAS

DRYADVM SILVAS, SALTVSQVE SEQVAMVR INTACTAS . VIRG .

A Netherlandish engraving of 1564 showing a dryad with her oak tree.

The supreme god and ruler of the heavens, Zeus was symbolized by thunder and lightning, and his chief weapons were thunderbolts, with which he expressed his anger. His Roman equivalent, also known as Jove, with the epithet 'Tonans', became Jupiter the Thunderer. In Shakespeare's *The Tempest* Prospero in his magic robes declaims his powers, among them

107

> To the dread rattling thunder
> Have I given fire, and rifted Jove's stout oak
> With his own bolt.[1]

As the god of thunder, Jupiter had counterparts: in Estonia, Uku; in Finland, Ukko; in the ancient Celtic world, Taranis. The oak features in Norse mythology too, being sacred to Thor, the god of the sky and thunder. He was said to ride through the sky in an oak chariot and his temples had tall oak pillars representing him. Thor carried an enormous magical axe-hammer, symbolizing thunder and lightning. Like Zeus, he was a divine protector of the community. His Old German, and hence Anglo-Saxon, counterpart was Donar. The belief that Thor sheltered under an oak tree during a storm gave rise to the household practice of keeping an acorn on a windowsill or carved on a banister to ward off lightning. Hence, the story goes, acorn-shaped pulls came to be fitted to window blinds. A more significant belief was in a battle between the oak king and the holly king, ending on the winter solstice, the longest night of the year, from which

The replanted oak at the shrine of Dodona, Greece.

St Boniface felling a sacred oak, 723 CE, in stained glass from a church in the Rhineland.

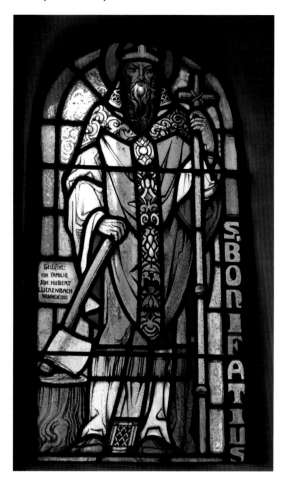

the oak king emerged as the victor. Called 'Yule', from a Scandinavian term meaning 'wheel', the turning of the wheel of life was a pagan occasion for a feast, when in the depth of winter people could look forward to lengthening days.

The Slavic equivalent of Zeus and Thor was Perun, the chief god in the pagan pantheon of Eastern Europe, and especially Russia. As the god of thunder and lightning riding in a chariot pulled by a goat, his weapons were an axe, a hammer and thunderbolts. In Slavic mythology, the world was represented by a sacred tree, usually an oak. Its branches represented the living world, the sky and the people who lived beneath it; the roots the underworld, the place of the dead. Perun, about whom there was considerable folklore, ruled over the living world, watching over mortals. Large oaks, sacred groves and other places were named after him, and goats and bulls were sacrificed to him at such sites. From 988 CE, when Vladimir the Great, ruler of Kievan Rus, converted to Christianity, hundreds of oak statues sacred to Perun were dragged through the mud, beaten with sticks and dumped in the Dneiper and other Russian rivers. Nevertheless, churches incorporated some of his characteristics in their saints, the Eastern Orthodox Church choosing the Old Testament prophet Elijah and the Roman Catholic Church choosing St Michael.

Saint Vladimir, as he became, had a German antecedent for persecution of the pagan oak in the English missionary and martyr St Boniface (*c.* 675–*c.* 754), who in 723 angrily cut down the holy oak tree, the Donareiche (Donar's Oak), near Geismar, south Germany, to prove to the heathens who worshipped it that Christianity was superior. As part of his campaign against the Saxons, who venerated the Irminsul (meaning 'Great Pillar') as the symbol of their chief god, Tiu (also known as Saxnot), the Frankish king Charlemagne (*c.* 742–814) had a great Irminsul destroyed. Practical benefits of oak trees were not ignored though. A ninth-century Benedictine monk at Malmesbury Abbey, Wiltshire, advised: 'To grow your herbs well and good you should keep them in raised beds with oaken sides', the point being that medicinal herbs of Mediterranean origin should not get too wet. The practice continues today in numerous re-created gardens.

In Celtic beliefs the most sacred tree was the oak, which represent *axis mundi*, the centre of the world. The Celtic name for oak was *daur*, the origin of the word 'door'. In a personal sense it can mean the way into one's inner thoughts and spiritual understanding, promoting growth as a human being at one with nature. Mythologically, the root of the oak was regarded as the doorway to the Otherworld, and the tree deities Darona/Daronwy were the god/goddess of the oak grove. A Druid, also related to the word *daur*, was one of the philosopher-priests practising during the Iron Age in Britain, Gaul and Ireland, one who was oak-wise, learned in tree magic and a guardian of the doorway. The door was not considered a place of endings but of new beginning, of reincarnation as occurred in the plant world of death, and rebirth. Such beliefs meant it was not difficult for outsiders, notably Roman writers, to look askance upon these ceremonies and to perceive their practitioners as sorcerers. In *Historia Naturalis*, Pliny the Elder (23–79 CE) describes a central part of one of their religious ceremonies:

> The druids – that is what they call their magicians – hold nothing more sacred than the mistletoe and a tree on which it is growing, provided it is Valonia Oak . . . Mistletoe is rare and when found it is gathered with great ceremony, and particularly on the sixth day of the moon . . . Hailing the moon in a native word that means 'healing all things', they prepare a ritual sacrifice and banquet beneath a tree and bring up two white bulls, whose horns are bound for the first time on this occasion. A priest arrayed in white vestments climbs the tree and, with a golden sickle, cuts down the mistletoe, which is caught in a white cloak. Then finally they kill the victims, praying to a god to render his gift propitious to those on whom he has bestowed it. They believe that mistletoe given in drink will impart fertility to any animal that is barren and that it is an antidote to all poisons.[2]

A common name of mistletoe, which grows not only on oaks, was Druids' herb. It was supposed to be the most efficacious remedy for a number of ailments, among them epilepsy, infertility and ulcers – that it could be found on oaks, made it all the more significant.

In *The White Goddess* (1948) the poet Robert Graves (1895–1985) dwells on the significance of the oak tree in Celtic mythology. He noted that in the ancient Welsh myth *Cad Godden* (The Battle of the Trees) are the lines:

> With foot-beat of the swift oak
> Heaven and earth rung;
> 'Stout Guardian of the Door'
> His name in every tongue.[3]

The Celtic word for door, sometimes spelt *duir*, has similar spellings in all Indo-European languages, the actual wood being the material for an entrance. The oak tree flowers in midsummer, the time of another turn in the seasonal wheel, as the anthropologist of religion Sir James Frazer, pointed out in *The Golden Bough* (1911–15), a work named after the golden bough in the sacred grove to Diana at Nemi, central Italy. It was on Midsummer Day that the human sacrifice of the Celtic oak-king Nemi took place, oak being the fuel of the fires burned during this ritual. The seventh month, at the midpoint of the thirteen lunar month calendar, began on 10 June and ended on 7 July. Midway came on St John's Day, 24 June, the day on which the oak-king was 'burned alive' and a funeral feast held in his honour. While the sun appeared to stand still fires danced. The smoke of green oak was painful, as the traditional 'Song of the Forest Trees' records:

> Fiercest heat-giver of all timber is green oak;
> From him none may escape unhurt.
> By love of him the head is set an-aching,
> By his acrid embers the eye is made sore.[4]

Burning it was supposed to inspire dancing on the occasion, the faces of the dancers painted black, the colour of lightning-struck oak.

The churches were not above aligning some of their events with and adopting elements of pagan beliefs and practices. For example, in the Roman Catholic Church the pontiff (from the Latin word *pontifex*, meaning 'bridge-builder') assumed the role of Jupiter, the link between heaven and earth, but without thunderbolts. In the transition from paganism to Christianity, much knowledge of nature and folklore was lost, to be recovered centuries later by researchers exploring the continuity of traditions, but regardless of this, the old ways helped smooth the process of conversion. It might have been something as simple as building a primitive church, convent or monastery on or near the site of a familiar oak. St Brigid of Kildare (*c.* 451–525), who became one of Ireland's patron saints, had the same name as one of the most powerful pagan goddesses.

From the mid-twentieth century, anthropologists such as Claude Lévi-Strauss (1908–2009) began laying out their theories of structuralism, regarding cultural elements in 'binary oppositions' as part of a total system rather than discrete beliefs. The pagan/ Christian dichotomy was an excellent example of structuralism, an underlying common structure built up from basic contrasts. A similar idea had been occasionally recognized in the Middle Ages when the Catholic Church, having acquired considerable temporal power and wealth, could accommodate what would well have been considered opposition. In 1505 Pope Julius II visited Viterbo and its sanctuary, where a miraculous image of St Mary of the Oak was venerated. The image got its name from the fact that a peasant hung it upon an oak tree; talk of it performing miracles such as healing, the granting of grace and deliverance from the plague attracted an increasing number of visitors. A few years later, the local thirteenth-century church dedicated to St Nicholas was restored and consecrated to Santa Maria della Quercia. Julius II had an oak as his heraldic symbol and wanted to diffuse the image of the Madonna della Quercia in Rome. In the Madonna della Quercia near Bassano in Teverina, the trunk of an oak tree is built into the altar.

Maria Taferl, a small market town and the most important pilgrimage site in lower Austria, is a place of pagan and Christian significance. In the local church plaza is Opferstein, a Celtic rock on which human sacrifices were believed to have been made. The original church was built around a shrine to the Virgin Mary. According to legend, the pietà at the shrine was offered by a forester, Alexander Schinagel, as a thanksgiving for a remarkable recovery from a serious illness. It replaced a crucifix on the site of another medical miracle. A local shepherd, Thomas Pachmann, tried to chop down the oak on which the crucifix was mounted, but in doing so he was badly injured in both legs. He prayed to the Virgin Mary, whereupon his near-fatal wounds stopped bleeding. The sumptuous Baroque church was completed in 1710, becoming a place of pilgrimage, especially for the cure of illnesses. It was over a holm oak at Fatima, Portugal, that Our Lady appeared to three children in 1917.

Oak men were not simply workers in forests; in folklore they were fairy folk, mischievous spirits who inhabited the woods. Later, in illustrations to children's stories they were depicted as wearing red toadstool caps or the tops of acorns as hats. They were said to spring up when a cut oak stump sprouted suckers. Beyond the colourful characters appealing to children, though, there was a more sinister story: wanderers were often told to be wary of going down to the woods at night, when oak men tempted the unwary with fairy food. This consisted of poisonous fungi and if too much of it was eaten at once, especially if the ingredients were fresh instead of being dried, then those who had made a meal of it could be driven insane. One way of neutralizing fairy folk magic was to turn your coat or cloak inside out:

> Turn your clokes
> For fairy folks
> Are in old oakes.

Another method of keeping the oak men at bay was, it was said, to help them to bury acorns by moonlight. The origin of the folklore seems not to have been in worship of the moon goddess, but in some of the long-established and widely spread mushroom cults, followed among others by shamans. Cults were based upon red- and white-capped hallucinogenic mushrooms which, suitably prepared and taken in small doses, could open the doors of perception. They may have been taken as part of a ceremony, an initiation or fertility rite, or an order to begin a hallucination leading to spiritual insights. Parallels have been drawn between mushroom cults and the Christian ceremony of the Eucharist.

Death and resurrection are represented in the image of the Green Man, to be found on three continents: parts of Asia, Europe and North Africa. It is an image of contrasts. Both pagan and Christian, it is known to have been used in Mesopotamia from around 3000 BCE and in can be seen western European medieval churches and cathedrals such as those at Canterbury and Chartres. The work of woodcarvers, stonemasons and painters, it can be seen above choir stalls, in roof bosses, on pew ends, pillars and plinths, in stained glass windows, inside and outside buildings, and on pub signs. Dressed in keeping, the Green Man takes part in May Day revelries welcoming the first day of spring. A merging of frontal face with tree foliage, the image is a fusion of the human and botanical. Sometimes the human face becomes leaves; branches and leaves may emerge from the sides of the mouth; more extremely, they spring from its eyes and ears as well as the mouth, perhaps twining round and back into the head; simply it may be a head framed by foliage. Different woods are featured: hawthorn, maple, mulberry, oak. Its 'voice' has been likened to the hiss of high wind in oak and ash. Vine leaves, bunches of grapes and ivy suggest a link with Dionysus, the Greek god of wine. The image is known under various other names: Jack in the Green, the Old Man of the Woods, or Puck.

A modern Green Man by master woodcarver Chris Pye makes a
distinctive house sign.

The nearest to the Green Man in the flesh is Peter the Wild Boy,
who was found in 1725 living a feral life in woodland in Hanover.
Believed to be about twelve, he had probably been abandoned by
his parents; he lived on grass and leaves, moved naked on all fours and
could not speak. On the order of George I, who became King of
England in 1714, but, not having learned English, spent most of his
time in Hanover, Peter was brought to England and given his name.
He aroused considerable curiosity and was written about by, among

others, the satirist Jonathan Swift and the journalist Daniel Defoe. In a painting of George I's court by William Kent, Peter is shown in a green velvet coat (he had to be wrestled into it) and holding oak leaves and acorns in his right hand. He was eventually retired to a Hertfordshire farm, where he died in 1785.

Venturing into the supernatural, Kingsley Amis (1922–1995) wrote a novel, *The Green Man* (1969). Set in a fourteenth-century pub, it was described by one reviewer as 'three genres in one: ghost story, moral fable and comic novel'. In all its manifestations, the theme of green features heavily with its connotations of freshness, fertility, new life, growth and decay – death to be followed by rebirth, as sure as spring follows winter.

Peter the Wild Boy with a handful of acorns and oak-leaves, painted by William Kent.

Not everybody appreciates trees. There are sufferers from dendro-phobia, fear of trees. It is a phobia often kept hidden because the sufferer fears ridicule. Yet for the individual it is very real, manifest in shortness of breath, rapid breathing or increased heart rate; sufferers avoid trees or flee in panic from what they regard as an inimical environment. The fear may be associated with tall or large trees that threaten to fall, especially if the wind gets up or a thunderstorm looms, a dense concentration of engulfing trees, or a tree that has a particularly painful association. It may be traced to a traumatic child-hood experience, such as seeing a frightening film featuring trees. Medication only masks the problem; cure of what is irrational involves understanding the root cause and coming to terms with it. Related to dendrophobia but less well known are hylophobia (fear of forests), nyctohylophobia (fear of dark wooded areas or forests at night) and xylophobia (fear of wooden objects).

Attitudes to oak say much about national character. A prime example is Germany, where in the eighteenth century Romantics looked back to an idealized Middle Ages which they saw as an unspoiled world of forests and heroes. The poet Friedrich Klopstock (1724–1803), more interested in northern than classical mythology, encouraged adoption of the oak as a national symbol. As Simon Schama writes in *Landscape and Memory*, 'The promised triumph of German greenery over Latin masonry produced a virtual oak-fetish in the art and literature of the late eighteenth and early nineteenth centuries.' He recounts a scene in which

> a group of students at Göttingen University, under the spell of Klopstock's tribal Druids, spent a night beneath the moon and stars in what was said to be an ancient oak grove. With their hands linked by garlands made of oak leaves, they swore eternal friendship and fraternity and con-stituted themselves a *Hain-Bund*, literally a 'Grove-League',

from which their druidical odes would seek to rejuvenate their Fatherland.[5]

Lohengrin (1848), the tale of the Swan Knight set in opera by Richard Wagner, includes a great oak, the Tree of Justice. Part of the inspiration for Wagner's *Ring* cycle (1848–74) came from the Icelandic *Völsunga Saga* legend. In the centre of the hall of King Völsung stood the great oak Branstock, the saga tells us. Disguised as a beggar the Norse god Odin, the protector of kings and brave young heroes, sank his sword up to the hilt in Branstock with the challenge that only he who could draw it out would own it. Only Völsung's son Sigmund was able to do it. In the early nineteenth century the oak, long rooted in folk memory, became the national tree of Germany.

A double oak is the symbol of Schleswig-Holstein, emphasising the inseparability of the two German regions. 'Teures Land, du Doppeleiche' ('Dear Land, You Double Oak') carries the same message in song. The Niedersachsenl ('Song of Lower Saxony') contains the lines 'Firm as oaks we stand / When storms rush across the German Fatherland . . .'. Oaks or oak leaves have appeared on generations of German coins: the Goldmark, Reichsmark, Deutschemark and pfennig, and now the euro. The 50-pfennig featured a woman planting an oak seedling, while an oak twig appears on German 1-, 2- and 5-cent euro. Other European countries also made use of oak leaves, for

The Tamme-Lauri oak on an Estonian banknote.

example in Italy on the 20-lire coin and Poland on the 2 grosze. The reverse of the Estonian 10-kroon banknote depicts Tamme-Lauri, the nation's oldest tree.

In 1936 potted oak seedlings were presented as a gift from the German people to each of the gold medal winners at the Berlin Olympics. The tree was closely associated with the Nazi Party, the oak crown being its symbol. It was a looking back to Teutonic tree worship and the classical world when garlands of oak leaves were an honour: in Shakespeare's *Coriolanus* the Roman general's mother says of him, 'To a cruel war I sent him; from whence he returned, his brows bound with oak',[6] a sign of victory. Insignia with oak leaves marked various Nazi honours. Heinrich Himmler, a fan of Arthurian legend and Wagner and later head of the SS, personally bestowed the *Totenkopfring* ('Skull Ring') upon officers; a silver ring worn on the third finger of the left hand as though it were a wedding ring, it had several runes and oak leaves topped off with a death's head. Inside was engraved the recipient's last name, the date of the award and Himmler's signature. Oak leaves with swords and diamonds to the Knight's Cross were instituted in 1941; only 27 were awarded, Field-Marshal Erwin Rommel being one of the recipients. The Hitler Youth badge of honour also featured oak leaves. Hitler's personal bookplate comprised an eagle, swastika and oak leaves. Hitler had a plantation near his birthplace, Branau am Inn, Austria, from which several hundred tiny oaks were taken to be planted throughout Germany and other occupied territories on his birthday, 20 April. Ceremonies, at which attendance was compulsory, often featured speeches extolling the promise of acorns, the deep roots of the oak and comparing its longevity to the Thousand Year Reich— which was to last just over twelve years.

The successful commando raid July 1943 to rescue the Italian dictator Mussolini, sacked by King Victor Emmanuel and held under house arrest, was dubbed Operation Eiche. Oak came to the aid of

Hitler's bookplate with German eagle and oak leaves.

Hitler when German officers led by Colonel Claus von Stauffenberg, hoping to overthrow the regime and secure a negotiated peace with the Allies, made an attempt on the Führer's life at a meeting on 20 July 1944. A briefcase bomb was left under the large oak table, but when it detonated one of the table's heavy oak supports shielded Hitler from the blast. Only injured, he had the satisfaction of savage reprisals being inflicted on some 150 alleged conspirators and fifteen senior Nazis committing suicide. Had the plot succeeded it could have shortened the war, saving thousands of lives. After the Second World War, 177 surviving senior Nazis, amongst them Hermann Göring, former commander-in-chief of the Luftwaffe, were tried at Nuremberg, the city where Hitler had held mass rallies and the anti-Semitic Nuremberg Laws were compiled. The accused were in an oak dock, made especially for the trials by U.S. engineers, to answer charges of crimes against humanity. The armrests were deliberately designed so that the accused could not sit too comfortably.[7]

French generals' kepis have a ring of gold oak leaves.

France made a more restrained use of the oak as a symbol. For example, franc coins featured an oak and olive crown; gold oak leaves decorated the band of the kepi worn by French officers; on the *Légion d'honneur* under the Third Republic (1875–1946) the crown was replaced by a laurel and oak wreath; in 1953 the emblem of France included an oak branch, symbolising wisdom; and on the *Ordre national du Mérite* instituted by President Charles de Gaulle 1963. The character of the tree was personified in the tall figure of de Gaulle (1890–1970), who restored national pride after three generations in which France suffered defeat in the Franco-Prussian War (1870–71), great losses on her own battlefields in the First World War, and an early defeat (1941) in the Second World War. He became the leader of the Free French and on 25 August 1944 triumphantly entered liberated Paris, embodying the spirit of France as a nation with a glorious past to be restored and a significant role to be played in shaping post-war Europe. The day after his death his commanding figure, drawn as a fallen oak, appeared on the front page of the centre-right newspaper *Le Figaro*.

In 1971 André Malraux, appointed Minister of Information by de Gaulle in the post-war government, published *Les Chênes qu'on Abat* ('The Fallen Oaks') based on his conversations with de Gaulle. De Gaulle's legacy lived on through the political party Rassemblement pour la République (RPR). In 1999 Michèlle Alliot-Marie won the election for president of the party, the first woman to lead a major French political party. In 2002 RPR merged with the Union for a Popular Movement (UMP), whose symbol is a white oak in the centre of upright blocks of blue and red, forming a resemblance of the Tricolour.

Edmund Burke (1729–1797) used apt metaphors in *Reflections on the Revolution in France* (1790) to emphasize French ignorance of the English character:

> Because half a dozen grasshoppers under a fern make the field ring with their importunate chink, whilst thousands of great cattle, reposed beneath the shadow of the British oak, chew the cud and are silent, pray do not imagine that those who make the noise are the only inhabitants of the field; that, of course, they are many in number; or that, after all, they are other than the little, shrivelled, meagre, hopping, though loud and troublesome insects of the hour.

In 'A Tree Song', Rudyard Kipling (1865–1936), patriot and imperialist, wrote:

> Of all the trees that grow so fair,
> Old England to adorn,

Greater are none beneath the Sun
Than Oak and Ash and Thorn.

Readers could be forgiven for thinking that these trees are in some way exclusive to England, forming part of the image of 'Merrie England' along with roast beef and ale. The oak is in fact the national tree of many countries, including the three Baltic states (Lithuania, Latvia and Estonia having had the oak god Perkūnas), Bulgaria, Moldova, Poland, the Basque Country (Janicot was the Basque oak god), England and Wales, France, Germany, Serbia, and the USA. Oak is America's most widespread hardwood, with some 60 species across the country, and is recognized by Congress as the nation's favourite tree. A live oak is the state emblem of Georgia and the official tree of the state of Iowa, which has twelve oaks native to it. An uprooted oak was the emblem of World Refugee Year (1959) drawing attention to the plight of refugees displaced from their homes and calling for a special humanitarian effort to help them.

In heraldry it occurs widely in family coat of arms, such as in those of the Scottish clans Hamilton, MacAndrews and MacEwan. Three acorn sprigs, one for each of the three children in the Middleton family and also representing their home county, Berkshire, are prominent in the coat of arms awarded to the family in 2011 before their daughter Kate married Prince William. The insignia of the U.S. Surface Warfare Medical Corps are gold metal pins with a spread oak leaf and other ornaments, to distinguish sections of the Corps. Senior officers in the Canadian Army have a row of gold oak leaves across the forward edge of their peaked caps and generals two rows, as does the Governor General of Canada as commander-in-chief of the Canadian armed forces. In the UK, the centre of the cap badge of the Cheshire Regiment is an acorn between oak leaves. A bronze oak leaf emblem was introduced for British soldiers 'mentioned in despatches' between 4 August 1914 and 19 August 1920; it was normally worn on the ribbon of the Victory Medal.

A U.S. Federal Reserve crest.

In the past the use of oak symbolism was not always so overt. When the court painter Steven van Herwijck painted Queen Elizabeth I in 1563, she wore a dress with oak leaves on it; to those who appreciated the symbolism it referred to the coat of arms of her lover Robert Dudley, Earl of Leicester. The crown manufactured for the coronation of Catherine the Great of Russia included oak leaves and acorns in small diamonds.

The Democratic Federation, founded in 1881 and eventually changing its name to the Social Democratic Federation in 1884, was the first socialist political body to exist in Britain. Its membership card, designed in 1882 by the utopian socialist William Morris, had as its motif an oak tree with abundant acorns and foliage in which hung banners

One of Elizabeth I's dresses, with oak leaves on the arm.

carrying the injunction 'Educate, Agitate, Organise' underneath the assertion 'Liberty, Equality, Fraternity'. An oak leaf is the symbol of the National Trust, the British charity founded in 1895 to preserve places of historic interest or natural beauty for the benefit of the nation. It was not until 1935 that it held a competition to design a symbol representing its activities. A prize of £30 attracted 109 entries, none of which was thought suitable, so a further competition was held with entry restricted to six invited designers. A further restriction was that the design should be based on, rose or oak, each readily associated with English heritage. The winning design was a short branch of green oak leaves against a pale background that would be easily recognized. Its designer was Joseph Armitage (1880–1945), who had produced decorated carvings for St George's Chapel, Windsor Castle, the Bank of England and South Africa House. On the centenary of the founding of the National Trust, the Royal Mail issued a set of commemorative stamps, of which the 25-pence stamp depicted an oak seedling.

With something as widely dispersed, geographically and historically, as the oak, its meaning has become diffuse. It means different things

An oak branch is the centrepiece of the National Trust logo. Here it directs visitors to the first property acquired by the Trust, Alfriston Clergy House, East Sussex, in 1896.

to various people over time, gaining and losing attributes. Moreover, the significance of a single tree can change, even within a short time. In Ettersberg, north of Weimar, there was an oak named after the German poet, dramatist and scientist Johann Wolfgang von Goethe (1792–1832), who had a mystical feeling for nature. He believed that the natural environment constructed a human being, and vice versa. Whoever walked every day under oak trees would become a different kind of person from somebody who walked under airy birch trees. A romantic, he was reputed to sit under a particular oak and pen his poetry. And in the mid-nineteenth century it became a site for the literary tourist to visit. Like Goethe, people believed that as long as the oak survived, Germany would flourish.

In 1937 a concentration camp for political prisoners was established in the relatively invisible forest nearby at Buchenwald, literally 'beech forest'. Goethe's oak was incorporated within the camp. Under orders, the inmates – socialists, communists, Jews, criminals and vagrants – chopped down the trees, but the oak was considered sacrosanct. Even though the oak was dying because its roots were starved of water, prisoners could imagine that Goethe was still there in spirit and occasionally enjoy its shade. Some of the bodies of the 56,000 men, women and children who were murdered there hung from its branches. On 24 August 1944, when Allied forces were moving into Germany, an incendiary bomb hit the tree and burned it down. Prisoners quickly chopped up the ruined tree for firewood, leaving the stump. It was an omen that the Third Reich would soon fall. From some of the wood rescued from Goethe's oak, as a memorial to the suffering and death of the Buchenwald prisoners, the author Bruno Apitz managed to sculpt a death mask, 'The Last Face'. The original is in Berlin and a copy in the Buchenwald Museum. Just before American forces liberated the camp, there was an uprising. It was regarded as the centre of the Communist resistance to the Nazis, central to the identity of the German Democratic Republic, the new communist state of East Germany established in 1949. Within just over a decade Goethe's oak had had four different identities. In 1960 the stump became the centre of the memorial to those who were imprisoned on the site.

Similarly, an oak stands within the most notorious of the Polish death camps, Auschwitz, on the right of the entrance gate with its metal sign bearing the slogan, 'Arbeit mach frei' ('Work sets one free'). Another silent witness is the oak at Oradour-sur-Glane, the village in central France where on 10 June 1944 members of the Waffen-ss murdered 642 men, women and children. The town has been left exactly as the troops left it. In the ruin, the only thing now flourishing is the oak.

So firm are the attributes of the oak, so adaptable its symbolism, that there are only a few minor superstitions associated with it. The rarely achieved eightieth wedding anniversary is symbolized by oak. It was also considered to have a healing property: driving a nail into the tooth or gum until it bled and then driving it into an oak was thought to transfer the pain from the sufferer to the tree. Fingernail clippings and leg hairs stuffed in an oak hole bunged up with cow's dung was said to get rid of gout. The operation for ague, an acute fever, was more painful: a lock of the sufferer's hair was pegged into an oak; a sudden wrench left both ague and hair behind. To stay healthy for a whole year, some Welsh believed you should rub an oak with the palm of your left hand. What sounds like an old wives' remedy made its way into the *Philosophical Transactions of the Royal Society* in 1672: 'To strengthen the Limbs by anointing them with Oyl, drawn out of the white Oak acorns'.[8] A Tudor treatise reckoned that a branch of mistletoe was a protection against evil;[9] similarly, if hunters cut an oak branch and with their dogs stepped over it they would be protected against witchcraft;[10] and a Scottish Highlander could protect himself against the fairy folk by drawing a circle round himself with an oak sapling.[11] May dew gathered under oak was especially effective.[12]

Contents of oak apples were used in divination. An ant within signified a good harvest; a white worm, murrain in cattle; a spider, a pestilence among men;[13] a little worm flying away meant wars; a creeping worm foreshadowed a poor harvest; an active worm, the plague.[14] In Wales a worm inside an oak apple was a sign of future poverty, but what the tree was not guilty of was causing poverty of the imagination.[15]

seven

Stature

The oak carries great meaning, it is respected, loved, and has been worshipped. Even today, in an industrial and urban society, where we have largely lost touch with nature and the seasons, there are 'tree huggers'. More than any other tree, the oak has helped people define themselves.

In *Le Docteur Pascal* (1893), his final novel in the Rougon–Macquart series, Emile Zola (1840–1902) has the doctor explain his family tree to his niece Clotilde with the despairing verdict:

> Look at our family tree. It covers only five generations. It is no more important than a blade of grass in the human forest, vast and dark, of which the people are the great secular oaks.[1]

Often the tree was a boundary marker, there for all to see and so firmly rooted that, without reference to maps, which were rare, there was little room for dispute on where a county or parish began or ended. The tree defined one's home territory, important when location could make a difference to one's obligations to the church (for example in payment of tithes) and community. A great oak was a place where locals could celebrate, joining in the party after church ceremonies by dancing around the tree. Where a tree had reached a prodigious age and been hollowed out, people wanting to mark some event in an unusual way might dine inside it.

Oak trees were landmarks where people gathered, a focus for a community with a common interest. Large enough to accommodate a crowd, large trees attracted attention, swelling the number of listeners to a gospel preached or speech given. When George Fox (1624–1691), founder of the Society of Friends, or Quakers, arrived in New York, hundreds came to hear him, so he held his meeting in June 1672 under two large oaks in Flushing. The trees are no longer there, but the event is recorded in a memorial stone on the site. In the Botanic Garden in Washington, DC, the Crittenden Oak marks the spot where John J. Crittenden (1787–1863), a senator from the divided state of Kentucky, made an address to try and avert the American Civil War. Planted by the senator, the tree native to Kentucky is known as 'the peace tree'. The garden also has a Chinese oak from the grave of the sage Confucius.

One unusual role for an oak was as a railway station house, as at Moreton-on-Lugg on the Shrewsbury and Hereford Railway, built between 1850 and 1853. Conveniently, its route took it by a hollow oak tree known locally as 'Eve', its fellow tree 'Adam' having been blown down in a gale. With a circumference of some 60 ft (18 m), as many as fifteen people were said to have taken tea in it at one time. When the railway was first constructed a navvy made his home in the hollow, which was given a thatched roof, a brick chimney and a fitted doorway. When he moved out the tree became a storehouse and lamp room. In 1862, when the railway was leased to the Great Western Railway (GWR), the tree became the home of the station-master and ticket office for Moreton-on-Lugg station. It was painted in the green and gold of the GWR and the roof re-thatched.

Oak can also be a living, growing reminder of an achievement. On 14 April 1961, two days after returning from man's first space flight, the Soviet cosmonaut Yuri Gagarin planted an oak in the Kremlin complex. Seven years later he was killed in an air accident and, reportedly, the tree fell sick, although it eventually recovered and flourished.

The Royal Oak, Crockham Hill, Kent.

Oak trees have also been places of refuge. In English folklore, they afforded shelter to the outlaw Robin Hood and his band in Sherwood Forest. The last great battle of the English Civil War was fought on 3 September 1651 at Worcester. Few escaped from the scene of carnage, but among them was the imposing figure of a dark-haired young man 'above two yards high', King Charles II. Proclamations were issued and a reward of £1,000 offered for his capture. With William Carless he hid in an oak tree at Boscobel in the neighbouring county of Shropshire before, disguised first as a woodcutter and then as 'Will Jackson', the servant of Jane Lane, being passed from one Catholic safe house to another and thence to the Continent, where he was to remain in exile for nine years. The oak became part of a legend and was named Royal Oak, later commemorated in many pub names with inn signs bearing the king's portrait. His birthday, 29 May, the day he entered London as the restored monarch in 1660 became Oak Apple Day, when the emblem of sprigs of oak with gilded oak apples was worn.

John Everett Millais, *The Proscribed Royalist*, 1853, oil on canvas.

The tree was a place where decisions were made. For instance, on the green in the small parish of Bonnington in Kent there is the Law Day Oak, where certainly since the late sixteenth century, and quite possibly earlier, courts heard local pleas. Today, in this settlement of some 100 residents, the annual parish meeting is still held under the oak. In 1889, a Mrs White wrote:

> Many rites and superstitions connected with the worship of the oak are still persisted in by the inhabitants. A special sacredness appertains to the vows of lovers exchanged beneath the Bonnington oak, and its leaves, gathered with a certain formula at a certain time of night, are still sought by childless women and made into a medicinal draught, with the same intention as in Druidical days.

A decision could be of international importance. In 1788, two friends of the same age who had met as undergraduates at Cambridge University, the Prime Minister William Pitt (1759–1806) and the philanthropist William Wilberforce (1759–1833), were discussing political moves. Wilberforce recorded the incident in his diary:

> At length, I well remember after a conversation with William Pitt in the open air at the root of an old tree at Holwood, just above a steep descent into the vale of Keston, I resolved to give notice on a fit occasion in the House of Commons of my intention to bring forward the abolition of the slave-trade.

This statement is engraved on the back of the stone seat on which Pitt the Younger and Wilberforce were sitting. Against powerful vested interests and preoccupation with the French Revolution and the subsequent Napoleonic Wars, the abolition was nearly twenty years coming. The slave trade was abolished in 1807, and slavery in 1833. The Wilberforce Oak, which toppled over in 1991, has since been replaced by a sapling.

James Gillray,
Tree of Liberty, 1798,
hand-coloured print.

The Tree of LIBERTY,. with, the Devil tempting John Bull.

The absence of plentiful oak timber was considered a serious situation that could adversely affect national standing. In Britain, by the beginning of Elizabeth I's reign (1558) a major shortage of timber was apparent. Demand for wood had grown with the increase in population. There were many calls on this natural resource, among them for buildings, tools, heating, trades dependent on fires such as baking and brewing, iron smelting and shipbuilding. In a period of inflation the price of wood rose sharply, far exceeding the general rise. Successive inquiry commissions reported on considerable deforestation in every county. On 15 October 1662 the diarist John Evelyn (1620–1706), who had been writing *Sylva*, a work on tree cultivation, following 'certaine Queries sent us by the Commissioners of his Majesties Navy', addressed the recently formed Royal Society on his concern regarding the supply of oak. The Dutch were the country's primary maritime rivals, and one of the roles of the British Navy was to keep open the trade routes to Baltic timber ports.

In France meanwhile, Jean-Baptiste Colbert (1619–1683), who became Controller General of Finances in 1665 and Secretary of State of the Navy in 1669, taking a strategic decision, enacted strict forest laws to ensure supplies of home-grown timber. His major investment was in the national Forêt de Tronçais, where he organized the planting of over 10,000 hectares of land, mainly with oak, especially tight-grained wood suitable for shipbuilding. He also persuaded Louis XIV that a new town should be built at Rochefort near the Atlantic coast, with a royal arsenal on the banks of the river Charente to construct, arm, supply and repair a war fleet. Its claim to fame came in the next century, however. In 1780 the Marquis La Fayette (1757–1834) embarked in the new three-masted light frigate *Hermione* on a 38-day crossing to Boston to support the Americans fighting for their independence from Britain.

In the late seventeenth and eighteenth centuries, leaving the Dutch and Spanish behind, France and Britain emerged as the most powerful European maritime nations. In their international rivalry Britain profited from its superiority at sea, gaining territories by war and peace treaties. In 1763, the year in which the Treaty of Paris ending the Seven Years War was signed, the shipwright Roger Fisher, of Liverpool published *Heart of Oak, The British Bulwark: Shewing* I, *Reasons for Paying Greater Attention to the Propagation of Oak Timber,* II, *The Insufficiency of the Ancient Laws . . .* IV, *That the Neglect of Planting . . . humbly offered to His Majesty and the Parliament, as well as to all proprietors of land in Great Britain.* Fisher's message was straightforward:

> And now by the happy revolution from popery, we are become a flourishing, free people; and by the happy union between England and Scotland, we are become one people; and as we have long been sensible that a maritime force is the strength of our nation . . . paying a more due attention to the propagation of that valuable part of our treasure, *the heart of oak.*

The welfare of our king and country, our religion, laws, and liberty depend upon it; for without the art of shipbuilding, and proper materials wherewith to construct ships, we shall soon become a prey to the next aspiring invader.[2]

The Seven Years War was timely evidence of the strength of his argument. Under the direction of William Pitt the Elder, Britain's actions had mainly been confined to actions at sea and in major overseas territories. The victories of James Wolfe in Canada and Robert Clive in India resulted in the conquest of Canada and the foundation of the Indian empire.

Shortage of oak in Britain had another effect of world significance. By the mid-seventeenth century smelting and forging using wood fuel was hampered by lack of resources. Iron masters, who already used coal in finishing processes, had to find ways of using coal, of which the nation had plenty, in furnaces and forges. By the latter part of the eighteenth century an energy resource above ground began to give way to a more powerful one from below. Increased use of coal was a contributory cause of the Industrial Revolution, which began in Britain and in turn led to the transformation of what, for millennia, had been primarily agricultural and craft societies.[3] In their place would be growing towns based on factories and mills, in which workers kept pace with machines producing goods en masse. Much of the landscape would be transformed in several ways, notably with a green and pleasant land becoming disfigured by dark satanic mills.

In times of adversity there is something defiant about the wood of an oak. The oak tree of Guernica in the Basque Country had been a symbol of local democracy since the Middle Ages, since it was where the laws of the Biscay region were drawn up until 1876, each town and village in the province sending two representatives to the

The Guernica oak, a place of Basque public assembly in the town
bombed by the Germans in 1937.

assembly. On 26 April 1937, during the Spanish Civil War, Nazi Luft-
waffe planes, in support of the Fascist dictator General Francisco
Franco overthrowing the Republic, bombed Guernica for nearly four
hours. This trial of blitzkrieg tactics – used further in the Second
World War– devastated the town and killed, according to official
Basque figures, 1,654 civilians. However, the oak survived.

Oaks have also historically been places to dispense justice. Near the palace of Louis IX (1215–70), nicknamed 'Saint Louis', was a grand oak with wide-spreading branches, under which the king sat in summer. There he received anybody, rich or poor, with a complaint to make. Complainants were allowed to tell their stories without hindrance while King Louis listened patiently for hours before doing what he could to right the wrongs.

A decision to plant a tree in memoriam has much to recommend it. The qualities of an oak can be seen to match the character of the deceased. In Britain the National Memorial Arboretum includes 2,535 oaks for over 45,000 British merchant seamen and fishermen lost in twentieth-century conflicts. Unlike a memorial stone, oak is a living, growing plant, with one hopes a long life. Now that cremations are common the tree can be planted, with the ashes of the deceased if desirable, in a setting that had a meaning for the individual. It is naturally suitable for a woodland burial.

The oak at Oradour-sur-Glane, a village destroyed by the Waffen-SS in 1944 and left thus as a memorial.

The French king Louis IX passing judgement under an oak at Vincennes.

One of the trees chosen as a focal point in the design of a Japanese garden, a haven of peace and tranquillity, is the oak. It makes for meditation. The tree is not so much a subject in itself as the provider of an atmosphere of quiet contemplation in which the imagination can flourish. Walt Whitman (1819–1892), for instance, was inspired to write in free verse one of his songs of male intimacy and love, 'I Saw in Louisiana a Live-Oak Growing':

> For all that, and though the live-oak glistens in Louisiana
> Solitary in a wide in a wide flat space,
> Uttering joyous leaves all its life without a friend
>   or lover near,
> I knew very well I could not.

Mark Twain wrote his first great success, the short story 'The Cele-brated Jumping Frog of Calaveras County' (1865) under an oak in Tuolumne County, California. In 1897 Twain stayed for two months in Weggis on the north shore of Lake Lucerne in Switzerland. During his stay he often sat on a bench and smoked under an oak tree. A plaque, mounted in stone, records 'Mark Twain Ruhe' (meaning 'took a rest'). His relaxed time is not linked to a specific work, but at least he recharged his creative energy. W. Béran Wolfe makes the point in an introductory essay to *The Pattern of Life* by the Austrian psychiatrist Alfred Adler (1870–1937):

> Each living organism has a definite life pattern and a definite and characteristic technique of combating the environment in order to maintain its life and goal. The complexity of the pattern varies with the organism's capability of change and adaptation, and for this reason the patterns of human behaviour are much more complicated than the pattern of an oak tree, a comparatively immobile and fixed organism.[4]

Camping under an oak before a battle served Andrew Jackson well on his way to the Battle of Horseshoe Bend, Alabama (1814): he eventually won a decisive victory over the Upper Creek Indians.

Two Americans found a rocking chair a good place in which to relax. When the house of Miss Maudie Atkinson, a maiden Alabama lady of about 50 in Harper Lee's Pulitzer Prize-winning novel *To Kill A Mockingbird* (1960), was burning down and neighbours were rescuing her belongings, the lawyer Atticus Finch carried out her heavy oak rocking-chair, saving 'what she valued most'. On medical recommendation, John F. Kennedy, suffering from a back injury sustained when the Japanese blew his torpedo boat apart in the Second World War and recovering from an operation in 1955, tried a rocking-chair. Made of Appalachian oak in North Carolina, its chief feature was a steam-bent curve in the back. This allowed his muscles to move, contract and relax while giving his back firm support. So impressed with the comfort was Kennedy that the chair was carried on to Air Force One when he was travelling and another was bought for the presidential retreat at Camp David. Others were installed in the family estates, given to friends and heads of state.

Meditation can be acute in the presence of an old oak, as it was for Prince Andrei in Tolstoy's *War and Peace* (1864–9):

'Yes, he's right, a thousand times right, the old oak,' thought Prince Andrei. 'Others, young creatures, may be caught anew by that deception, but we know life – our life is over!' A whole fresh train of ideas, hopeless, but mournfully sweet, stirred up in Prince Andrei's soul in connection with that oak. During this journey he thought over his whole life as it were anew, and came to the same hopeless but calming conclusion, that it was not for him to begin anything fresh, that he must live his life, content to do no harm, dreading nothing and desiring nothing.[5]

Six weeks later, when the oak has burst into leaf, Andrei realizes that his life is not over.[6]

Reflection on the old age of a tree is particularly acute if it is a shadow of its former self: broken, decayed, supported by crutches, a mere stump. A plaque can add poignancy to a relic, prompting thoughts of past associations, glories and tragedies, speculations on the events to which it has been a silent witness. Trees talk only in tales, but they do stimulate the imagination. An old tree is not only part of our heritage; it is also living history. Hence it is well worth preserving for as long as possible, which was the aim of Dr Edwin Lewis Stephens when he founded the Live Oak Society in the U.S. in 1934. According to the by-laws of the Society only one member is human, the chairman; all the other members, from the president down through the vice-presidents are registered live oaks. Membership qualification is a girth of eight feet or more and one with a girth of over sixteen feet is classified as centenarian. Beginning with 43 members, the Society now has over 6,000 members, named after people or places in fourteen American states. The largest registered stand, of 249 live oaks, is in City Park, New Orleans.

The oak has a certain standing, whether or not it was standing at the time it was named. Its roots may be in legend. The original may have been felled, its site taken by a replacement or merely a memorial, an informative plaque or stone. In an art form it may have a continuing future. Herne's Oak in Windsor Great Park, to the west of London, makes the point. In fact there have been three successive trees of the same name there. The most notable mention of Herne's Oak is in Shakespeare's comedy *The Merry Wives of Windsor* (c. 1600):

> There is an old tale goes, that Herne the Hunter,
> Sometime a keeper here in Windsor Forest,
> Doth all the winter-time, at still midnight,
> Walk round about an oak with great ragg'd horns;
> And there he blasts the tree, and takes the cattle,
> And makes milch-kine yield blood, and shakes a chain
> In a most hideous and dreadful manner.
> You have heard of such a spirit, and well you know
> The superstitious idle-headed eld [old men]
> Receiv'd, and did deliver to our age,
> This tale of Herne the Hunter for a truth.[7]

The plot of the comedy is based on enticing the knight Falstaff to come to Herne's Oak at night 'disguised like Herne, with huge horns on his head'. This is based on an older folk tale. The legend of Herne is of a huntsman in the service of Richard III (1377–99), who saved the king's life but was branded a thief by other huntsmen. Out of royal favour, he was found hanging from an oak tree. Other suggestions for the origin of the character go back further: Herne is associated with Hermes, the messenger of the gods in Greek mythology; for the Celts he is derived from their deity Cernunnos; the Norse link is to Woden, who led the wild hunt.

More numerous are the appearances of Herne's Oak in music, literature, on TV and elsewhere, including in versions of the Robin Hood legends. When Ted Hughes (1930–1998), poet of nature, became

The actual 'Herne's Oak' in Windsor Great Park.

poet laureate in 1984, one of his obligations was to mark state occasions. The task of producing official poetry on a given theme to a deadline is not always relished by poets; their effort can easily descend into verse. For the Queen Mother's 95th birthday in 1995, Hughes wrote 'The Oak Tree', in which he compared her to a six-rooted tree. The work did not meet with universal acclaim. Hughes also collected oak items, new and old, large and small. One of them was a snuff-box, found in a junk shop. which was one of the carved mementos

An engraving, after Fuseli, of Sir John Falstaff at Herne's Oak in
Windsor Great Park, from *The Merry Wives of Windsor; c.* 1805.

made from the timber of a Herne Oak felled or brought down by a gale. In 1977, after ten years of composition he produced 'Gaudete', a long poem intended as a film scenario about the double of a vicar, a modern fertility god who seduced village wives and was hunted down and killed by their outraged middle-class husbands. In a narrative of sex, violence and death, reminding us of Dionysian excesses, it can be regarded as a harsh view of contemporary civilization, a way of life that has lost its essential link with nature. Much of the significance of ancient folklore and customs has been obscured in sanitized rituals, even lost.

The past of the oak is secure in buildings, incidents, names, paintings, places, songs, stories and much more. In a changed world with modern materials and many different priorities, there is no guarantee of the long-term attraction of the wood and the status the past accorded it. No more than a historic relic, on our more densely populated planet it risks being relegated to the margins of society, the preserve of but a few dedicated conservationists.

eight

The Arts

With so many practical uses over such a long history and so much weighty symbolism, changing with circumstances, it was natural that oak would have a role in a number of art forms. It has formed design features in places as distant as Buddhist gardens in Kyoto and English eighteenth-century country estates. Saiho-ji is a Zen Buddhist temple famous for its carpet of moss, encouraged by the branches and leaves of pine, maple and oak partly shutting out sunlight. Where sunlight shines through on to the moss, it makes it glow in a tranquil green-gold light. During the Kamakura period of Japanese garden design (1150–1310), the emphasis was on a stately tree, a focal point to attract attention. Landscape gardeners set out to create a beautiful view. In England, Lancelot 'Capability' Brown (1716–1783) imported trees such as evergreen oak and had them planted strategically; Humphry Repton (1752–1818) experimented by planting several small trees together in the same hole, as many as nine oak seedlings, so that the trunks would fuse together. What looks like a large box hedge from above in the Bandini garden in Frascati, Italy, is in fact a rectangle of 200-year-old holm oaks carefully trimmed to reveal a shady avenue of straight trunks. In the American South a preferred site for a stately antebellum plantation house was in a clump of mature oaks, providing natural, cooling shade. The legacy of planting and conserving trees lives on. A recreational sport of climbing mighty oaks with harnesses is practised in the U.S., the UK and Japan.

Some nine trunks are fused together in the Repton Oak planted about 1815 in Reservoir Wood, Essex.

Oak is an art material in its own right. It can be painted or gilded and until the sixteenth century, when canvas became the more popular medium, flat panels of it were the basis of paintings, in the Middle Ages mainly of religious subjects. The panel had first to be treated with glues and resin and covered with linen, and then a smooth plaster surface created. Oak panels were widely used in Europe: in Italy, France, the Netherlands, northern Germany, Denmark and Norway. Notable artists who adopted it included Leonardo da Vinci (1452–1519) when he was employed by the king of France; Albrecht Dürer (1471–1528) in the Netherlands and southern Germany; and Hans Holbein the Younger (1497–1543) when working in southern Germany and England. Lesser known is the Flemish artist Ambrosius Benson (c. 1495–1550) who, for instance, produced a portrait of Mary Magdalene in oils on an oak panel. The fact that paintings were done on oak panels has led to considerable work being done on their dating by dendrochronology in tandem with radio-carbon methods, notably at the Research Laboratory for Archaeology and the History of Art at Oxford University and the Institute for Wood Biology at Hamburg University. Researchers set out to establish the earliest possible date or the number of years over which the work was executed and also the provenance of the wood. For example, much of the wood used by Dutch and Flemish artists in the Netherlands, which was short of oak from the fifteenth to the seventeenth centuries, originated in the Baltic and was exported from the Polish port Gdańsk.

A specialized form of oak panel was the icon, an image of a religious subject and itself regarded as sacred and an object for worship. A typical example of the subjects depicted was the story of Abraham and his wife Sarah, who lived in an oak grove in the plains of Mamre. According to Genesis 18:2, they were visited by three men, whom they entertained with a specially prepared meal. The Old Testament version of the Holy Trinity was one of the icons that became an aspect of Holy Russia from the seventeenth century. Religious mysticism was a dominant principle in Russian life through to the end of the nineteenth century. The last Tsar of Russia and of the Romanov dynasty, Nicholas II (1868–1918) and his wife Alexandra had a large

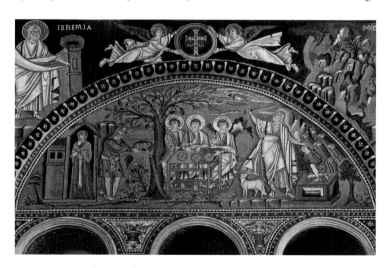

The Oak of Mamre as depicted in a Ravenna mosaic.

collection of icons, 130 of them hung closely on the walls of their room. The couple prayed to them daily.

Paintings of oaks as subjects in themselves date mainly from the seventeenth century onwards. In the early rooms of Nijo Castle, Kyoto, the home of the first shogun, built in 1603, there are paintings of thick, dark oaks with warlike animals, including leopards and birds of prey, intended to intimidate visitors. The seventeenth century was the Golden Age of Dutch landscape painters. Jan van Goyen (1596–1656) was a prolific artist who began his work with an oak panel, choosing natural subjects such as in *Landscape with Two Oaks*.

Jacob van Ruisdael (*c.* 1628–1682), from a family of landscape painters, was primarily a painter of trees, giving loving attention to details of foliage, as in *Oak Tree and Dense Shrubbery at the Edge of a Pond* and *The Great Oak*. *The Watermill Oak* by his pupil Meindert Hobbema (1638–1709) is often reproduced and he was a formative influence on the

Jan van Goyen, *Landscape with Two Oaks*, 1641, oil on canvas.

Jacob van Ruisdael, *Oak Tree and Dense Shrubbery at the Edge of a Pond*, mid-1640s,
oil on wood.

Jean-Baptiste-Camille Corot, *The Forest of Fontainebleau (The Oak)*, 1834, oil on canvas.

Theodore Rousseau, *The Oak among the Rocks*, 1856–60, oil on panel.

Ivan Shishkin, *Oak Grove*, 1887, oil on canvas.

English Romantic artist John Constable (1776–1837). The main sketching ground of the French landscape painter Jean-Baptiste-Camille Corot (1796–1875), influenced in turn by Constable, was the forest of Fontainebleau, rich in oak trees. A contemporary of Corot, Theodore Rousseau (1812–1867) was also attracted to the site and influenced by Constable, producing among other similar paintings *A Group of Oaks at Apremont in the Forest of Fontainebleau* (1855) and *The Great Oaks of Old Bas-Beau* (1864).

Landscape painting preserving relaxed, pastoral scenes flourished in the eighteenth and nineteenth centuries. Thomas Gainsborough (1727–1788), best known as a portrait painter, started his career by copying Dutch masters with rural scenes such as *Cornard Wood* (1748). He was influenced by Ruisdael and progressed on to a series of landscapes that include *A Wooded Landscape with a Herdsman Reclining near a Weir* (1753) and *A Landscape with Gypsies* (1753–4). Around 1758 he produced a self-portrait with oak leaves in the background. The career of the Scottish painter Alexander Nasmyth (1758–1840) was the reverse; it began with portraits and ended with landscapes. His son Patrick (1787–1831), whose best-known work is *Sir Philip Sidney's Oak* (1820–30), came to be called 'the English Hobbema'. Trees held a similar fascination for the Russian landscape artist Ivan Shishkin (1832–1898). Among his works conveying the atmosphere of forests are *Oak Grove*, *Oaks – Evening: A Study* (both 1887) and *Rain in an Oak Forest* (1891).

Oak is an expressive material, a natural choice for sculpture. Indeed, it can be carved naturally, by the action of the elements. Driftwood examples are admired and sold, like hand-carved oak, such as the sculptures by Jacopo della Quercia (*c.* 1374–1438), they have a particular permanence. Oak seems to encourage experiment. Paul Gauguin (1848–1903), best known for his paintings, produced some oak sculptures in later life: a pair of clogs in polychrome oak and leather (1889–90); *A Woman with Mango Fruits* (1889) was produced in carved and painted oak; *Lewdness* (1890), a gilded and polychrome oak, pine and metal sculpture; and in 1894, a bas-relief on oak, *Pape Moe* (*Mysterious Water*).

German performance artist Joseph Beuys (1921–1986) had a concept of social sculpture, summed up in his famous statement 'Everyone is an artist.' Working together, he believed that people could change their environment and hence society itself. In 1982 he delivered 7,000 blocks of basalt to Kassel Town Hall and arranged then in a large arrow pointing to a solitary oak he had planted outside the building. With the slogan 'Stadtverwaldung statt Stadtverwaltung' ('City Afforestation instead of City Administration'), visitors were encouraged to take away a block and in exchange plant an oak elsewhere. The project, 7,000 Oaks, was a success – over the next few years all the trees were planted across the city.

A piece of conceptual art that continues to divide art lovers and critics alike is Michael Craig-Martin's *The Oak Tree* (1973). It consists of a glass of water on a shelf and a wall-mounted text. The artist explained that the work is

> a full-grown oak tree . . . It's not a symbol. I have changed the physical substance of the glass of water into that of an oak

Stephen Taylor, *Oak in Early Spring*, 2005, oil on canvas.

tree. I didn't change its appearance. The oak tree is physically present, but in the form of a glass of water.

Having a Catholic background, Craig-Martin makes an analogy with the idea of transubstantiation, the belief that bread and wine, while looking just the same, are transformed into the body and blood of Christ. His act of faith was not universally understood. While Damien Hirst praised it,[1] the sculptor Anthony Caro commented: 'Some of the stuff that's called art is just damned stupid. I mean "That glass of water's an oak tree" kind of thing.'[2] The art critic Giles Auty's observation expanded upon the division that the piece created among observers:

Stephen Taylor, *Oak and Wheat*, 2005, oil on canvas. In these paintings of a pedunculate oak, images of permanence and rebirth, Essex artist Stephen Taylor condenses themes of the landscape: the sky above everything, property boundaries, modern industrial crops and ancient native trees. He has painted this tree over 50 times in three years.

> How would [a critic] react if, on ordering oak planks for an
> outhouse, he were sent instead a bucketful of water? Would
> he gently muse on 'the subtle and obscure waters of identity'
> – or make immediate reflections on the mental well-being
> of his timber suppliers?[3]

With its open grain and tendency to tear, oak is not the easiest of
woods to carve; however, modern tools make carving it easier and can
give finer detail. Its sister art, pyrography – burned-wood etching –
does not work well because the wood itself gets dark. Far from being
in decline, both arts are flourishing, with creative standards much

Q: To begin with, could you describe this work?
A: Yes, of course. What I've done is change a glass of water into a full-grown oak tree without altering the accidents of the glass of water.
Q: The accidents?
A: Yes. The colour, feel, weight, size …
Q: Do you mean that the glass of water is a symbol of an oak tree?
A: No. It's not a symbol. I've changed the physical substance of the glass of water into that of an oak tree.
Q: It looks like a glass of water …
A: Of course it does. I didn't change its appearance. But it's not a glass of water. It's an oak tree.
Q: Can you prove what you claim to have done?
A: Well, yes and no. I claim to have maintained the physical form of the glass of water and, as you can see, I have. However, as one normally looks for evidence of physical change in terms of altered form, no such proof exists.
Q: Haven't you simply called this glass of water an oak tree?
A: Absolutely not. It is not a glass of water any more. I have changed its actual substance. It would no longer be accurate to call it a glass of water. One could call it anything one wished but that would not alter the fact that it is an oak tree.
Q: Isn't this just a case of the emperor's new clothes?
A: No. With the emperor's new clothes people claimed to see something which wasn't there because they felt they should. I would be very surprised if anyone told me they saw an oak tree.
Q: Was it difficult to effect the change?
A: No effort at all. But it took me years of work before I realized I could do it.
Q: When precisely did the glass of water become an oak tree?
A: When I put water in the glass.
Q: Does this happen every time you fill a glass with water?
A: No, of course not. Only when I intend to change it

into an oak tree.
Q: Then intention causes the change?
A: I would say it precipitates the change.
Q: You don't know how you do it?
A: It contradicts what I feel I know about cause and effect.
Q: It seems to me you're claiming to have worked a miracle. Isn't that the case?
A: I'm flattered that you think so.
Q: But aren't you the only person who can do something like this?
A: How could I know?
Q: Could you teach others to do it?
A: No. It's not something one can teach.
Q: Do you consider that changing the glass of water into an oak tree constitutes an artwork?
A: Yes.
Q: What precisely is the artwork? The glass of water?
A: There is no glass of water any more.
Q: The process of change?
A: There is no process involved in the change.
Q: The oak tree?
A: Yes. the oak tree.
Q: But the oak tree only exists in the mind.
A: No. The actual oak tree is physically present but in the form of the glass of water. As the glass of water was a particular glass of water, the oak tree is also particular. To conceive the category 'oak tree' or to picture a particular oak tree is not to understand and experience what appears to be a glass of water as an oak tree. Just as it is imperceivable, it is also inconceivable.
Q: Did the particular oak tree exist somewhere else before it took the form of the glass of water?
A: No. This particular oak tree did not exist previously. I should also point out that it does not and will not ever have any other form but that of a glass of water.
Q: How long will it continue to be an oak tree?
A: Until I change it.

Michael Craig-Martin, *An Oak Tree*, 1973.

David Nash,
Cracking Box,
1990, oak.

above those of the era of popular pokerwork texts of homely philosophy. On the face of it chainsaw carving is a cruder and quicker art,
practised by performance artists and suitable for garden sculptures
seen at a distance. Here again, finer implements can fashion detail.
The sculptor David Nash has combined carving and fire, for instance
in *Large Oak Throne* (1997), a piece of charred oak from a single tree
exhibited in a woodland setting. A fine example of miniature carving
is a 47-inch (120 cm) model of Nelson's flagship HMS *Victory* carved
from a piece of oak from the lower gun deck of the original ship. The
original timber, removed during restoration work, was so hard that

at times the sculptor, Ian Brennan, felt it was like carving concrete, making the work longer to complete than imagined: seventeen years. In meticulous detail it includes 104 guns, 37 sails and 200 ft (60 m) of rope. Also carved out of a single piece of oak is a statue of Nelson's ultimate enemy, Napoleon, imported from France in 1822. Now in the Merchant Adventurers' Hall, York, its original purpose was to advertise snuff, of which Napoleon was fond.

Oak trees are very visual objects and inspire not just painters and sculptors. An oak can even become a film set in its own right, especially if it is convenient to Hollywood, as happened to the Hooker Oak in Chico, California. The tree is named after the English botanist and director of the Royal Botanic Gardens, Sir Joseph Dalton Hooker (1817–1911) who, when he saw it for the first time, declared it to be 'the largest of its species in the known world'. In 1921 it was 110 ft (35 m) tall. It was estimated that, on the basis of one person occupying an area of 2 ft² (0.2 m²) per person, 7,885 people could stand under its canopy, big enough to pass for a forest in itself. In the Oscar-winning film *The Adventures of Robin Hood* (1938), Errol Flynn formed his outlaw band beside the Hooker Oak.

The Swedish aerial photographer Jocke Berglund was flying over Småland, when he saw a large oak tree-shaped print on the ground below. A distinctive yellow-red image, it had been created by a combination of a hurricane flattening the local pine forest and the imprint left by logging machinery. The image made Berglund Wildlife Photographer of the Year 2006.

Over the years oak has appeared in the titles of a number of plays, for the most part now not much played. Examples include *Hearts of Oak* (1879) by James Herne and David Belasco, Sean O'Casey's *Oak Leaves and Lavender* (1945), a propaganda play about the Battle of Britain; and *Fumed Oak: An Unpleasant Comedy* (1936), a short play by Noël Coward, features an oppressed middle-aged salesman who frankly tells his wife, mother-in-law and 'horrible adenoidal daughter' what he thinks of them and walks out. More frequent than titles are references to the tree in the context of individual characters and situations. It often appears in relation to death. In Shakespeare's *Cymbeline* (*c.* 1610), when Cloten has been killed by Cymbeline's lost sons Guiderius and Arviragus, they sing 'Fear no more the heat o' the sun', a song about death that includes the line 'To thee the reed is as the oak'.[4] Similar associations also occur in poetry. Ben Jonson (*c.* 1573–1637) comments on the brevity of life and its pleasures:

> It is not growing like a tree
> In bulk, doth make men better be;
> Or standing long an oak, three hundred year,
> To fall a log at last, dry, bald, and sere.[5]

The poet John Donne (*c.* 1571–1631), when Dean of St Paul's Cathedral, preached on the subject:

> It comes equally to us all, and makes us all equal when it comes. The ashes of an Oak in the Chimney, are no epitaph of that Oak, to tell me how high or how large that was; It tells me not what flocks it sheltered while it stood, nor what men it hurt when it fell. The dust of great persons' graves is speechless too, it says nothing, it distinguishes nothing.[6]

In 'The Talking Oak' by Lord Tennyson a tree talks to a young lover:

> For oft I talk'd with him,
> And told him of my choice,
> Until he plagiarised a heart,
> And answer'd with a voice.
>
> Tho' what he whispered under Heaven
> None else could understand;
> I found him garrulously given,
> A babbler in the land.

The fall of an oak can be dramatic, as Tolstoy relates near the end of *Anna Karenina* (1873–7):

> Lowering his head and battling against the wind, which was tearing the rugs out of his hands, Levin had almost reached the wood and already caught sight of something gleaming white behind an oak, when suddenly there was a blinding flash and the whole earth seemed to have caught fire and overhead the vault of heaven seemed to crack. Opening his blinded eyes, he saw with horror through the curtain of rain the strangely altered position of the green crown of a familiar oak in the middle of the wood. 'Has it been struck?' he thought. The thought had barely time to cross his mind when, gathering speed, the top of the oak disappeared behind the other trees and he heard the crash of the great tree falling on the others.
>
> The flash of lightning, the peal of thunder, and the sudden sensation of cold that spread over his body merged for Levin into one feeling of horror.
>
> 'Dear Lord, dear Lord, not on them!' he said.[7]

He rushes to see what has happened to his wife and son, but he finds them unharmed.

American-born Isabella Burt (1841–1911) in the first chapter of *Memorials of the Oak Tree, with Notices of the Classical and Historical Associations Connected with It*, published in London in 1863, heaped praise on the tree. She wrote,

> One of the most stately ornaments of our woods and forests is the Oak Tree. Of the vegetable productions so profusely bestowed upon us, there are few that can be compared with, and none to surpass, this truly regal tree for beauty, durability, strength and usefulness. It is as truly the monarch of the forest as the lion is king of the beasts.[8]

John Ruskin, *A Spray of Dead Oak Leaves*, 1879 (both the study and a watercolour and bodycolour painting on paper)

Caspar David Friedrich, *Oak Tree in the Snow*, 1829, oil on canvas.

The treatment of fine oak timber in Jerome K. Jerome's novel *Three Men in a Boat* (1889) was enough to make one of the characters aghast. Visiting a house in Kingston on the River Thames, he is shown a handsome carved oak staircase, of such quality would have done credit to a palace. The oak panelling leads all the way up to a drawing room, where he finds the panelling covered in blue wallpaper.[9] Popular books had the wood as a background feature, for example *The Whiteoaks of Jalna* by the Canadian novelist Mazo de la Roche (1879–1931) and Georgette Heyer's *Royal Escape* (1938), about Charles II fleeing Cromwell's men by hiding in the Royal Oak. The naval novels of C. S. Forester (1899–1966), charting the rise of Horatio Hornblower, and those of Patrick O'Brian (1914–2000), are set in the Napoleonic Wars, when the wood was still the basic material for British naval vessels.

Literary characters named after oak tend to reflect the characteristics of the wood. For instance, Gabriel Oak in Thomas Hardy's *Far From the Madding Crowd* (1874) is a solid, dependable man, unaffected by disaster and unselfishly protecting the impulsive and wilful Bathsheba. Beset by problems, he considers emigrating, but decides to stay and overcome them, which he eventually does. Similarly, Dorinda Oakley in Ellen Glasgow's *Barren Ground* (1925) determinedly faces her situation and deals with it. The daughter of poor parents who scraped a living from a dirt farm in Virginia, she sees her escape and a better life in marriage, the hope of most young women. But it does not work out that way: the man she falls in love with seduces and then jilts her. Pregnant and alone, she has the strength of a Presbyterian conscience and 'the vein of iron held in her soul'. Oakley does not look for a man to rescue her or the sympathy of others. Like George Bernard Shaw's 'New Woman', she chooses work instead of passion, for 30 years putting her energies into making the barren ground pay. Glasgow's character becomes a success as an independent woman, lacking happiness but able to hold her head high as one with the virtues of integrity and endurance.

A piece of oak furniture was enough to hang a story on for Victorian and Edwardian readers. In 1850 George Payne James (1799–1860), a prolific author popular in circulating libraries, published a three-volume novel, *The Old Oak Chest: A Tale of Domestic Life*. In 1905 Emily Taylor used the simple device in *The Old Oak Chest: A Book of Great Treasure*, a tale of two children finding in grandmother's attic a chest containing old clothes. After dressing up, they find a book of stories at the bottom of the chest, which their grandmother told them a girl had written. The children enjoyed reading them instead of making a noise to upset grandma.

'An enormously important dwarf' in J.R.R. Tolkien's *The Hobbit* (1937), Thorin Oakenshield, so called because when his shield was damaged he used an oak branch as protection, comes to respect Bilbo Baggins after gaining a bad first impression of his smaller hobbit accomplice. Thorin is also mentioned in the successor novel *The Lord of the Rings* (1954–5). Worlds of fantasy fascinate children, taking them into a magical world of 'once upon a time'. This was well understood

Gustave Courbet, *The Oak of Flagey (The Oak of Vercingetorix)*, 1864, oil on canvas.

Claude Monet, *The Bodmer Oak, Fontainebleau Forest*, 1865, oil on canvas.

by Alexander Pushkin (1799–1837), who in his first successful romantic poem *Ruslan and Ludmíla*, immediately captures the imagination. Even
a prose distillation of the many verse translations engages the reader,
young or old. The prologue opens with this image:

> A green oak stands by the shore of a bay. Around the oak is
> a golden chain and by day and night a learned cat walks round
> and round on the chain.

The cat describes the wondrous things in the forest and the prologue
concludes,

> The spirit of Russia is there – a scent of Russia is in the air.
> And there I sat, drinking mead. I saw the green oak by the sea,
> and sat beneath it as the learned cat told me his stories. Some
> of these I remember, and I will tell them now to the world.

When Masha sings the opening words of Pushkin's poem under her
breath in the first act of Chekhov's *Three Sisters* (1901), Olga comments
that Masha is sad today. It is the name day of the third sister, Irina, who
will be having a party.[10]

Teryosha is a folk tale told by Aleksey Tolstoy (1883–1945), a distant
relative on his father's side of Leo Tolstoy. The boy Teryosha is captured by a witch, who wants him roasted for dinner, leaving it to her
daughter to do so. Teryosha turns the tables on her, pushing her into
the oven and escaping to the top of an oak tree. The witch returns, eats
her cooked daughter, relishing the meal, and then sees the boy in the
tree, which she tried to gnaw down. After breaking her front teeth,
she asks the blacksmith to make her some iron ones. Only with a
second set is she able to make the tree creak and sway. Teryosha pleads
to two flocks of flying geese to rescue him but they refuse, saying he
would have to ask the young goose coming behind them. The young
goose saves the boy, taking him home. *The Giant Oak Tree* is another
Russian fairy tale, similar to *Jack and the Beanstalk*. Other such stories in

which the oak features are *María Morvena*, *Masha and the Bear*, and *The Tsarevna Frog*. When Aleksandr Solzhenitsyn (1918–2008) decided to write his memoirs on his efforts to get his work published in his own country, he entitled it *The Oak and the Calf: Sketches of Literary Life in the Soviet Union*. The Russian title, translated literally reads: 'A Calf was Head-butting an Oak Tree', a wry image of his predicament.

Many children's stories featuring the oak are also favourites with adults. One such is *Lord of the Forest* (1975) by BB, a pen name derived from the size of the lead shot used by the author, naturalist Denys Watkins-Pitchford (1905–1990), when shooting geese. In the story, an eleven-year-old boy, Hugh Lambert, plants an acorn in Andreswald (the Weald); it is 1272, the year in which King Henry III died and was succeeded by Edward I. Showing his skill as an archer by killing a pole-cat, Hugh is rewarded by a man on horseback with a silver groat. Who could this big, rich man be, hunting in the king's preserve? Hugh later discovers he was 'Longshanks', the nickname of Edward I. Unhappily, the boy losses the coin he had been given. The book traces the life of the tree in that forest for nearly 700 years thereafter, its role in people's lives and the wildlife in and around it. In May 1944, troops in the area prepare for D-Day, the Allied landings on German-occupied France. As what might be a farewell link with his homeland an English soldier, another Hugh Lambert, plants what is unknowingly the last acorn from the giant oak in the hope that it will grow like the old one. In the hole he has dug he finds what at first he thinks is a sixpence; it is the thirteenth-century silver groat with the king's name in a Latin abbreviation.

A didactic tale like *Happy Pilgrim* (2007) by Czech writer Peter Bindes has a lesson more for adults than children:

> An old oak who lived in a grove loved to talk to animals and
> other trees. Answering a young oak's question about how he
> got to the grove, he explained that a soldier used to gather
> acorns and, after a victory in battle, plant one. 'I was the last in
> his pocket and that's how I came to be here.' The young oaks
> realised that they were the grandchildren of the old oak and

he was equally proud that they were growing up and flourishing. Remarking it was a pity that the soldier, after so many battles, was unaware of his legacy, prompted another question, 'Why do we oaks live so much longer than people, grandad?' Old oak's reply came after some considered thought, 'Most people live their lives in perpetual hurry. They're so busy rushing about they don't stop to appreciate what they've already got'. Which prompted another question from little oak, 'When they stop rushing about and relax will people live longer than us?' The answer was immediate, 'Yes, and maybe better too'. Which made little oak wonder how he in turn could advise people to live longer in the harmony of a peaceful world like the serene grove that was his home.

Oak trees have found a home in both classical and popular music. In the first act of Handel's (1685–1759) dramatic oratorio *Susanna* (1749), the second elder sings:

> *The Oak That for a Thousand Years*
> Withstood the tempest's might,
> Like me, the darted lightning fears
> And flames with sudden light.

The song 'Cinco Robles' ('Five Oaks'), written in Spanish and English with male and female singers alternating, is ideal for a duet performance, as was done for instance by Les Paul and Mary Ford. A folk song with English, Irish and Scottish origins, 'The Water is Wide', has been sung since the seventeenth century and appeals both to classical and popular tastes. Its theme is the lovelorn:

> I leaned my back up against a young oak
> Thinking he were a trusty tree
> But first he bended and then he broke
> Thus did my love prove false to me.

Vincent van Gogh, *Rocks with Oak Tree*, 1888, oil on canvas.

Franz Marc, *The Little Oak Tree*, 1909, oil on canvas.

'The Old Oaken Bucket' by Samuel Woodworth (1784–1842), a nostalgic celebration of scenes of childhood, has lines

> And e'en the rude bucket that hung in the well
> The old oaken bucket, the iron-bound bucket,
> The moss-covered bucket that hung in the well.

In 1826 it was set to music, to be sung by generations of American schoolchildren. 'The Brave Old Oak' by Henry Fothergill Chorley (1808–1872) also has a jaunty tune.

> Then here's to the oak, the brave old oak,
> Who stands in his pride alone!
> And still flourish he, a hale green tree,
> When a hundred years are gone!

There have been many variants of the original. Traditional English songs such as 'The Oak and the Ash' also focus on the tree:

> Oh! The oak, and the ash, and the bonny ivy tree,
> They flourish at home in my own country.

Much like the song 'The Royal Oak', about a naval encounter between the British and the Turkish, possibly in the seventeenth century, the oak continues to live on.

In the USA, the army marching song 'She Wore a Yellow Ribbon' seems to have had its origin in the English Civil War (1642–51), when the ribbon was part of Puritan dress. From there it crossed the Atlantic and, partly aided by the Western film by John Ford of the same name (1949), a yellow ribbon has become a symbol in the modern era with various meanings around the world. In America, expressed in the song 'Tie a Yellow Ribbon Round the Ole Oak Tree', it had the specific meaning in the nineteenth century of the woman waiting faithfully for the return of her man serving in the cavalry, and in the later twentieth century, from a jail term. A traditional dance song such as 'Coffee Grows on White Oak Trees', sung to the lively playing of a fiddle, has several variants across the nation. 'Saturday Night in Oak Tree Grove, Louisiana' is in the Cajun tradition. 'The Oak Tree' is a traditional Irish reel, while the Irish song 'The Dungarvan Oak' with its chorus, goes:

> Lay down your woolen shawl me love
> I swear it is no joke
> And I'll tell to you the story
>   Of the Old Dungarvan oak.

The name of the song's eponymous oak may well have had its origin in Wales, with the site of Caernarvon in the north of the principality or Carmarthen in the south. The words of 'Woodman, Spare That Tree' (1830) by the poet George Pope Morris (1802–1864), came about when the author by chance drove to the site near New York of an old oak planted by his grandfather that was about to be cut down. In 1837, when the poem was first published, an English pianist visiting America, Henry Russell (1812–1900), set it to music and it quickly became popular, now being claimed as an early ecological ballad.

Oak wood can be used to make a long lasting housing for organs. For instance, the organ of St Etienne Abbey in Caen, Normandy, needed replacing after it was destroyed by the Huguenots. Almost 200 years later, a master carpenter, Gouy from Rouen, built a monumental oak casework that was consecrated in 1745. It contained over 4,000 pipes, 60 registers and five keyboards. The instrument survived the French Revolution, partly through renderings of the Marseillaise at the right times. In the late nineteenth century, the working parts were replaced within the perfectly preserved casework, then valued at 60,000 francs; the new instrument cost 70,000 francs. Since 1975, the organ has been listed as part of France's cultural heritage.

Charles De Wolf Browne, *The Charter Oak*, 1857, oil on canvas.

The percussion instruments, xylophone and drums are often made of oak. The sound of a xylophone, literally 'wood voice', varies with the type of wood used: the denser the wood, the more authentic the sound. For example, Japanese white charcoal, *bincho-tan*, is harder than black charcoal and when struck it rings with a metallic sound. Wind chimes and the Japanese *tankin* (charcoal-xylophone) are made from it. For stability, tubular metallic bells are often mounted in an oak frame. Japanese oak is used in the manufacture of Yamaha drums for professional performances. Scrub oak is preferred for hi-tech drums, constructed from staves. A drum, or *taiko,* is struck with *bachi,* which can also be made of scrub oak.

In short, the wood has an accessible permanence in the arts. It has established an enduring place in the visual arts, music and literature, in both highbrow and popular culture. In that sense it can be regarded as post-modern.

nine

Conservation

Taking one's anger out on oak trees is a bizarre revenge for losing a football match. It is one of those news stories that sounds like spoof. The actual incident happened in Auburn, Alabama, where Auburn Tigers fans traditionally festooned two 130-year-old oaks with toilet paper ('tree rolling') to celebrate a victory over their arch-rival, Alabama Crimson Tide. In early 2011 the innocent trees were poisoned with lethal doses of the herbicide Spike 80DF, probably by some over zealous Alabama fan. Perhaps because the crime had gone unnoticed, a 62-year-old retired Texas State Trooper, Harvey Updyke, boasted to a popular radio show that he was responsible for the act of environmental vandalism. He was arrested and charged with criminal mischief.

Regarding the health of oak trees, there have always been diseases to combat, mildew being the most common. This covers leaves with a white film, in fact a fungus, as though Puck has been busy with a whitewash brush. It can reduce the strength of the tree, making it harder for it to survive in shade. Conversely, severe air pollution can act as a fungicide. Among other deleterious fungi is the one causing oak wilt. Many diseases are recent discoveries. Acute oak decline, encountered in Britain and Spain, manifests itself in dark fluid bleeding from slits in the bark. Believed to be caused by a previously unknown bacterium, it can kill a tree within four to five years. In

Oak processionary moth caterpillars making their way up an oak trunk.

sudden oak death, which is known to have occurred in the U.S. and Europe, the upper trunk also starts to bleed a black fluid through the infected bark before the foliage blackens and the tree dies. The cause is a fungus-like pathogen that causes lesions.

More widespread are the actions of moths, to which oaks are generous hosts, providing ample feeding zones. Caterpillars of oak leaf roller moths, for example, can cause severe defoliation. The oak processionary moth is so called because its caterpillars leave their nests in chains to make their way to the top of the tree, where they feed on the top leaves. With their voracious appetites, they defoliate the tree. Moreover, every caterpillar has over 60,000 toxic hairs that are a health hazard to humans and animals, causing skin rashes, itchy eyes and throats and bringing on asthma attacks. Native to southern Europe, they have been kept at bay by predators there, but with climate change they have spread north, where they have to be contained by insecticides or burning of their nests. A side effect of the 1987 gales in southern England and of 1999 in Europe has been an increase in the oak pinhole borer, a beetle that can penetrate the heartwood of oak logs. It does not affect standing trees.

There are organizations well equipped to research the causes and cures, or at least amelioration, of such diseases. In the UK there is the Forestry Commission, formed in 1919 when war had again prompted demands for more home-grown rather than imported timber; in the U.S.A the Department of Agriculture Forestry Service; and, concerned with global trends, the International Union of Forest Research Organizations, founded originally in 1892. Increasing attention is being paid to the impact of climate change on trees and what can be done to mitigate its effects. The role of trees in absorbing carbon is recognized, but perhaps not widely enough. About half the dry weight of a tree is made up of stored carbon, most of which is released when the tree rots or is burned. Trees also take in rainwater and store it, reducing potential damage by excessive rainfall and flooding.

Forests are more than sites of special scientific interest and recreation. United Nations agencies are aware of the importance of trees in economies, as sources of energy, as commodities in trade, and their impact on the environment. To raise awareness, the United Nations Forum on Forests designated 2011 the International Year of Forests.

Protecting is promoted. Just as New York pays farmers in the Catskills not to develop their land under the international scheme REDD (Reducing Emissions from Deforestation and Forest Degradation), on a larger scale developing nations are given financial encouragement to leave trees standing. REDD is financed by richer nations. An example of international co-operation in conservation is the bilateral arrangement between India and New Zealand to conserve oaks in the foothills of the Himalayas. Farmers habitually cut leaves and branches to feed their cattle and use the wood as fuel; New Zealand grows acorns and raises seedlings, which are sold for cash, which in turn is used to promote similar activities and encourage buying of trees in India.

Climate change, global warming in particular, has increased interest in phenology, the recording of recurring natural phenomena such as the first appearance of leaves and flowers. Once the pastime of amateur naturalists who noted dates from which seasonal and annual changes could be compared, historical climatology has now become a partnership between organizations and bands of volunteers. For example, Robert Marsham, a landowner who in 1736 began recording events in Norfolk, a county exposed to northerly winds, started a family tradition that continued until 1958. From the Marshmans' observations it was established that, in the long-term, the time of the year at which the oaks burst into leaf was becoming earlier. Data available in 1960 showed that over the last 250 years the first leafing date of oak had advanced by about eight days, suggesting an overall warming of 1.5°C over that period. Today there are phenology networks in Australia, Canada, China, Europe and the USA. The UK network is a cooperation between the Woodland Trust and the Centre for Ecology and Hydrology in Cambridge.

There is nothing unusual about violent storms, which often occur in the historical record. There was a week-long one in 1703 that struck with winds of over 120 mph (195 km/h), flooring 4,000 trees in the New Forest and 3,000 in the Forest of Dean. John Evelyn entered in his diary for 26 November:

The dismall Effects of the Hurecan and Tempest of Wind, raine and lightning thro all the nation, especialy London, many houses demolished, many people killed: 27 and as to my own losse, the subversion of Woods and Timber both left for Ornament, and Valuable materiall thro my whole Estate, and about my house, the Woods crowning the Garden Mount, and growing along the Park meadow; the damage to my owne dwelling, and Tennants farmes and Outhouses, is most Tragicall; not to be paralleled with any thing hapning in our Age [or] in any history almost, I am not able to describe, but submit to the Almight[y] pleasure of God, with acknowledgement of his Justice, for our National sins, and my owne, who yet have not suffered as I deserved to . . .[1]

At the end of the century in one of his letters, Edmund Burke summed up the feeling of devastation such an event leaves behind.

The storm has gone over me; and I lie like one of those old oaks which the late hurricane has scattered about me. I am stripped of all my honours; I am torn up by the roots, and lie prostrate on the earth![2]

Modern hurricanes such as Katrina, which hit New Orleans and the Gulf Coast in 2005, are equally devastating. High winds severely pruned many of more than 1,000 oaks in the City Park and, where seawater penetrated, roots were poisoned.

Against the mighty forces of nature, the efforts of mankind seem many but are, even collectively, no match. But people do not have to feel they have been relegated to the role of 'tree huggers', enthusiastic but impotent. Individuals can invest in the future by planting acorns. In an 1862 issue of the *Atlantic Monthly*, the American essayist Ralph Waldo Emerson (1803–1882) recalled his experience of learning from fellow writer Henry David Thoreau, who had lived much closer to nature:

A storm-felled oak in southern England.

When I was planting forest-trees, and had procured half a peck of acorns, he said that only a small portion of them would be sound, and proceeded to examine them, and select the sound ones. But finding this took time, he said, 'I think if you put them all into water, the good ones will sink'; which experiment we tried with success.

Emerson took the view that 'The creation of a thousand forests is in one acorn.' Useful information when it comes to raising seedlings for replanting. In the UK the planting of 1,600 trees by Chiswick House & Gardens Trust included the two species of native oak, woodland whips that were two years old, amid a ground mixture of hawthorn and hazel shrubs as the understorey.

On a national scale, the Woodland Trust is campaigning to plant 20 million trees of indigenous species by 2050. These species are classified as the 39 that survived the last Ice Age. It also has a project, the Ancient Tree Hunt, to map the location of trees 600 or more years old, the majority of them likely to be oak. The Trust points out that protecting ancient woodlands and creating new ones amounts to more than just a concern for trees as an end in themselves. They are unique habitats that are often threatened by development in the name of economic necessity and progress. What is the value of a woodland when measured against a new airport or high-speed railway line? Once lost, trees cease to be home for their many dependants: in the UK creatures such as the dormouse (extinct in over half its former range in Britain), red squirrel and lesser spotted woodpecker, to name just three of hundreds, many of them invisible or apparently unconnected. The long-term aim of preserving our heritage for future generations encourages initiatives such as those that volunteer harness to find and record ancient trees.

In 1998 at Tatton Park, a National Trust estate in Cheshire, a large oak nearing the end of its natural life was felled. Realizing that the wood could have more than its normal commercial value, two men had an inspiration: save and use all parts of the tree to create products. Under Project OneTree, sections were distributed to artists, crafts-people and manufacturers to make a range of beautiful and useful pieces. After a national touring exhibition the pieces were sold, creat-ing a financial legacy. Profits were set aside to create a new woodland. A suitable site near an existing woodland was bought, donations solicited for planting it and the Woodland Trust agreed to take on long-term management of what is part of the Mersey Forest. By the winter of 2004 the woodland was fully planted, with tourist and education schemes following. The National Trust, which has con-ducted a three-year survey (2009–12) of more than 40,000 ancient trees in its care, encourages creative use of wood felled on its properties. For example, woodturners and chainsaw carvers visit sites and in demonstrations, produce for sale objects such as garden ornaments and furniture.

In the U.S., where there is more land, there is greater scope for con-servation. A lead was given by George Washington who, soon after achieving victory in the War of Independence, returned to Mount Vernon, Virginia, where he wrote to contacts across the thirteen states asking for specimens of indigenous trees, emblems of the new nation. Among them were live oaks from the South, planted with other species in 1785 on his estate. A later president saw trees as an element in economic recovery. Under his Emergency Conservation Work Act of 1933, Franklin Roosevelt created the Civilian Conser-vation Corps. Like other public works projects, it provided work while profitably improving infrastructure and the environment. In Missouri in 1939, he established the Mark Twain National Forest, Twain having been born at Hannibal, by the Mississippi River. The forest, mainly within the Ozark Plateau in the southern half of the state and with an area of 1.5 million acres (6,100 km²), includes native oak, hickory and pine. Public work projects of this kind, providing immediate work, offering training in woodland management and building a green future, are essential in our climate-conscious century. Scars of development, for example mining and quarrying, can be landscaped and replanted, recreating a visually attractive landscape for visitors, which in turn leads to further opportunities. In southeast Missouri, Big Oak Tree State Park was established at East Prairie in 1937 to preserve some of the largest trees in the state, including

	Circumference	Height	Spread
Bur Oak	229″ (5.8 m)	154′ (47 m)	92′ (28 m)
Swamp Chestnut Oak	272″ (6.9 m)	156′ (47.7 m)	104′ (31.6 m)
Shumard Oak (d 1997)	205″ (5.2 m)	134′ (40.8 m)	86′ (26.2 m)

Another state rich in oaks, ten species of them, is California, the forests of which stretch into part of Mexico. A survey of California oak woodland, Oaks 2040, estimates that some 750,000 acres (3,000 km²) is under threat from population growth.

Governments can help conservation through a sympathetic tax regime. In the UK there are tax breaks for maintaining woodlands: no capital gains tax on their increasing value; no inheritance tax after two years of ownership. Individual trees can be subject to tree preservation orders, preventing them from being cut down, uprooted, lopped, wilfully damaged or destroyed, except with planning authority consent.

In the UK, the charity Plantlife, dedicated to saving wild plants, wants to make it an offence to plant alien intruders that may be attractive in gardens but, when they stray into the countryside, compete with native species. Among them are the Turkey oak and the evergreen holm oak. The Turkey oak, common in Europe from the time of the Ottoman invasions and in the UK since the eighteenth century, was first recorded there in the wild in 1905. It now invades nature conservation sites such as open grassland and heathland, which have their own ecosystems. In addition, it is a host of the

Oak apples caused by a cynipid gall wasp (*Biorhiza pallida*) on a pedunculate oak.

knopper gall wasp, an insect that from the latter half of the twentieth century has damaged the acorns of native English oaks. Of Mediterranean origin and an aggressive colonizer in southern England, the holm oak has been known in the UK for over 400 years, but was first identified in the wild in 1862.

Conservation is not always simple; there can be conservation conflicts. At the Polish estate of Rogalin, near Poznań, there are some 1,400 oak trees, regarded as 'nature monuments'. The older trees are also host to the great Capricorn beetle, one of the largest long-horn beetles in Europe. Under the EU programme Natura 2000, which should be preserved, the trees or the beetles? On the face of it the oaks are in

The Capricorn beetle (*Cerambyx* sp.) damages oaks badly beneath the bark.

The Capricorn beetle itself.

constant agony, evident in the broken bark clinging to them. However, the species of oak is very common in Poland, so it does not enjoy the same degree of protection as the great Capricorn beetle, which is in decline. The solution is to try and save the oldest and biggest oaks, keeping them healthy with organic fertilizers. In this way it is hoped that they will remain strong enough to tolerate the beetles feeding and multiplying at their expense – grubs of the beetle feed for as long as five years in the sapwood.

A long-term solution to the loss of plants through climate change and the pressures of human activities is the preservation of seeds. With world population expected to increase by 50 per cent by the middle of the twenty-first century, pressures on our environment will become even greater. Hence the importance of conserving seeds not just in their home countries, but also outside their native habitat. The world's largest plant conservation project, coordinated by the Royal Botanic Gardens at Kew, is the Millennium Seed Bank at Wakehurst, West Sussex. Here seeds are cleaned, dried and kept in large underground cold stores. This is not such a simple routine as it sounds, as Head of Research Professor Hugh Pritchard explains:

> All of the species in *Quercus* [oak] so far looked at have desiccation-sensitive fruits/seeds losing viability when dried below about 30% moisture content. In contrast, the seeds in our vault tolerate drying to about 3% moisture, which gives them considerable longevity in their dry state. There are likely to be many other seeds with the same biology as that seen in *Quercus* so we are trying to find ways to preserve them using very low temperatures – cryopreservation.

Taking the long view, the significance of conservation cannot be overestimated. The history of the oak as we know it begins in the most recent epoch in geological time, the Holocene, which began some 10,000 years ago with the retreat of the glaciers and a warmer climate in which vegetation could flourish. Geologists increasingly argue that the Holocene is giving way to the Anthropocene, the epoch in which man is having an unprecedented effect upon the environment. Global warming is but one aspect of this paradigm shift. A growing world population puts more pressure on resources of food and essential materials, as always unequally and unfairly distributed among the 7 billion inhabitants of the planet. Within this century world population could potentially increase to 10 billion.

In this scenario, the future of our forests and the fate of one tree in particular can seem a minor concern. The simple fact is that in the Anthropocene epoch, man is the major factor in determining the kind of environment and societies in which generations to come will live. Natural disasters will always occur but these pale into insignificance against deliberate plundering of the planet. We have only the one and space travel is more likely to export problems than solve them. In this context, trees can be seen as an investment, not just as a cash crop but also for the future of the planet. Not only do they add to the quality of the environment, increasing its diversity of plant and animal communities; they confer a practical benefit by absorbing carbon dioxide and maintaining cleaner air. They also add to the quality of life. A walk through woods can be a journey through natural history and the history of a homeland, the scented air stimulating the imagination. As W. H. Auden (1907–1973) put it in his poem 'A Culture is no Better than its Woods':

> The trees encountered on a country stroll
> Reveal a lot about a country's soul.[3]

Forests often have strong links with the past. None more so than Sherwood Forest and its association with Robin Hood. Every year in early December, a week of celebrations is held there for Tree Dressing Day, when some of the ancient oaks are decorated by local children as a mark of respect. All year round thousands of visitors come to see the Mighty Oak, thought to be 800 years old. What events have such trees lived through and survived, even taken part in? They cannot speak, like those in fairy tales, but they are powerful in conveying a definite atmosphere. Above all the oak, even when elderly and supported by crutches, stands out from all other trees in imparting a feeling of sound continuity.

Timeline

c. 10,000 BCE	Start of the Holocene. With melting of the ice sheets, forests grow in the northern hemisphere
c. 3,000 BCE	First image of the Green Man appears in Mesopotamia
2nd millennium BCE	According to the Old Testament, the oak is sacred to believers in the Lord
c. 2,000 BCE	Wooden 'henges' are built, reminiscent of sacred sites in forest clearings
1st millennium BCE	The shrine of Dodona, a sanctuary in Greece, based on a sacred oak tree, is gradually identified with Zeus
	Oak causeways and trackways improve land communications
Early 7th century BCE	Dugout canoes also serve as coffins. Succeeded by boats built of oak planks.
Iron Age	Furnaces for smelting are established
264 BCE – 5th century CE	Romans drove piles, built bridges, docks, ships
Early 7th century	Sutton Hoo ship burial
c. 1000 CE	Early Christian churches in oak. Islamic lattice-work carvings

Middle Ages	Timber-framed houses, barns and halls with hammer-beam roofs are built with oak
	Shakespeare's 'wooden O' Globe theatre is erected
16th–18th centuries	Rival building of 'wooden walls' to achieve naval supremacy in Europe. Shortages of oak timber
18th century	Development of inland waterways with oak-built locks
	John Harrison constructs his all-wood longcase clock
1716	Richard Arkwright's spinning machine, the first step in mechanizing the cotton industry, uses oak in its construction
1890	First electric chair, in New York State
2000	Millennium Seed Bank opens in UK
21st century	Growth of conservation movement as part of heritage, reducing carbon levels

References

1 Seeing the Trees

1 *New Scientist* (13 January 2011).
2 Isabella Burt, *Memorials of the Oak Tree* (London, 1863), p. 4.

2 Diversity

1 James Boswell, *The Life of Samuel Johnson* (London, 1791).
2 Toulmin Smith, *Parliamentary Remembrancer* (1861), p. 189.
3 William Plomer, ed., *Kilvert's Diary* (London, 1944), pp. 304–5.
4 John Dryden, *Palomon and Arcite* (1700) l. 1,058.
5 Joseph Needham, *Science and Civilisation in China* (Cambridge, 1996), vol. VI, p. 598.
6 Cyril Hart and Charles Raymond, *British Trees in Colour* (London, 1973), p. 26.

3 Home

1 Geoffrey Chaucer, *The Parlement of Foules* (c. 1380), line 176; Edmund Spenser, *The Faerie Queene* (1590), I, i, 8.
2 Grahame Clark, *Prehistoric England* (London, 1948), pp. 111–12.
3 Oliver Rackham, *The History of the Countryside* (London, 1986), p. 87.
4 Caroline Knight, *Essential Frank Lloyd Wright* (Bath, 2001).
5 Joseph Moldenhauer, ed., *The Maine Woods* (Princeton, NJ, 1974), p. 71.
6 G.M. Trevelyan, *English Social History* (London, 1946), p. 149.
7 Martyn Bramwell, ed., *The International Book of Wood* (London, 1976), p. 94.
8 G. Wickham, H. Berry and W. Ingram, *English Professional Theatre, 1530–1660* (Cambridge, 2000), p. 535.
9 Peter McCurdy, http://www.mccurdyco.com/globefab.html.
10 *History Channel* (19 July 2010).
11 Quoted by Edwin A. Pratt, *History of Inland Transport and Communications in England* (London, 1912), p. 144.

4 Away

1   Horace, *Odes*, I,iii.9.
2   V. Gordon Childe, *Prehistoric Communities of the British Isles* (London, 1949) p. 130.
3   Peter Marsden, *Sealed by Time: The Loss and Recovery of the Mary Rose* (Portsmouth, 2003), p. 19.
4   Jeremy Black, *Eighteenth-Century Europe* (Basingstoke, 1999), pp. 67–9.
5   Edward Paget-Tomlinson, *An Illustrated History of Canal & River Navigations* (Ashbourne, 1993), pp. 208–9.
6   Martin Walker, *Guardian Weekend* (London, 12 December 1981) p. 9.
7   Wilfred Owen and Ezra Bowen, *Wheels* (New York, 1969) p. 14.
8   Philip Wilkinson, *What the Romans Did For Us* (London, 2001), pp. 59–60.
9   Plutarch, *Lives*, trans. J. Langhorne & W. Langhorne (London, 1879), I, 8/I.
10 Oliver Rackham, *The History of the Countryside* (London, 1986), p. 92.

5 Wood in Words

1   William Cowper, *The Task* (1784), I.313.
2   W.S. Coleman, *Woodlands* (1866).
3   John Keats, *Hyperion* (1818–9), Book I. 72.
4   *The Odyssey*, (BookRags, Inc), Book XII, lines 25–7.
5   *The Aeneid*, trans. A.S. Kline, Book IV, lines 331–2.
6   R. S. Surtees, *Handley Cross* (London, 1843), I.xi.210.
7   Gerald Kersh, *Night and the City* (London, 1946) p. 27.
8   *Egil's Saga* (Icelandic Sagas), ch. 71.
9   Erasmus Darwin, *The Temple of Nature* (1803), canto 4, lines 347–8.
10 Cuthbert Bede, *The Adventures of Mr Verdant Green* (1853), ch. 4.
11 Charles Clover, *Daily Telegraph* (30 May 2008).
12 William Shakespeare, *King Lear* III. ii. 4–6.

6 Symbols and Superstitions

1   William Shakespeare, *The Tempest*, V. i. 45.
2   Pliny the Elder, *Historia Naturalis*, XVI, 95.
3   Robert Graves, *The White Goddess* (1948), p. 37.
4   Ibid., p. 210.
5   Simon Schama, *Landscape and Memory* (London, 1995), p. 103.
6   William Shakespeare, *Coriolanus*, I. iii. 16.
7   *The Guardian* (20 November 2010), p. 39.
8   *Philosophical Transactions* (Royal Society, 1672), 7, 5021.
9   Rembert Dodoens, *A Niewe Herball or Historie of Plantes*, trans. H. Lyte (London, 1578) p. 747.
10 Reginald Scot, *The Discoverie of Witchcraft* (London, 1584), XII, xviii.
11 Thomas Pennant, *A Tour in Scotland* (London, 1776), p. 46.
12 *Herefordshire Times* (24 May 1879), p. 13.

13 Dodoens, *Niewe Herball,* p. 746.
14 Thomas Lupton, *A Thousand Notable Thing, of Sundry Sortes* (London, 1579), III§7.
15 Marie Trevelyan, *Folk-Lore of Wales* (London, 1909), p. 101.

7 Stature

1 Emile Zola, *Le Docteur Pascal* (Paris, 1893), p. 118.
2 Roger Fisher, *Heart of Oak, The British Bulwark* (London, 1763), p. 7.
3 Henry Hamilton, *History of the Homeland* (London, 1947), p. 163.
4 W. Béran Wolfe in Alfred Adler, *The Pattern of Life* (London, 1931), p. 12.
5 Leo Tolstoy, *War and Peace,* trans. Constance Garnett (London, 1971), p. 449.
6 Ibid., p. 452.
7 William Shakespeare, *Merry Wives of Windsor,* IV.iv. 31–42.

8 The Arts

1 Damien Hirst, *Telegraph Magazine* (24 November 2007).
2 Anthony Caro, *The Guardian* (8 January 2005).
3 Giles Auty and Michael Craig-Martin, *encyclopaedia.com* (5 November 2008).
4 William Shakespeare, *Cymbeline,* IV, ii. 267.
5 Ben Jonson, *To the Immortal Memory . . . of . . . Sir Lucius Carey and Sir H. Morison.*
6 John Donne, Sermon xv (8 March 1621/2).
7 Leo Tolstoy, *Anna Karenina* (New York, 1961) p. 802.
8 Isabella Burt, *Memorials of the Oak Tree* (London, 1863) pp. 2–3.
9 Jerome K. Jerome, *Three Men in a Boat* (London, 1889), ch. 6.
10 Anton Chekov, *Three Sisters* (London, 1951) p. 98.

9 Conservation

1 John Evelyn, *The Diary of John Evelyn* (Oxford, 1985), pp. 423–4.
2 Edmund Burke, *A Letter to a Noble Lord* (1796).
3 W. H. Auden, *Bucolics,* II.

Further Reading

Bramwell, Martyn, ed., *The International Book of Wood* (London, 1976)

Hageneder, F., *The Living Wisdom of Trees: Natural History, Folklore, Symbolism, Healing* (London, 2005)

Harding, Mike, *A Little Book of the Green Man* (London, 1998)

—, *A Little Book of Misericords* (London, 1998)

Harris, E., Jeanette Harris and N.D.G. James, *Oak: A British History* (Macclesfield, 2003)

Hart, Cyril and Charles Raymond, *British Trees in Colour* (London, 1973)

Lewington, Richard and David Streeter, *The Natural History of the Oak Tree* (London, 1993)

Logan, W. B., *Oak: The Frame of Civilisation* (New York, 2005)

Pakenham, Thomas, *Remarkable Trees of the World* (London, 2003)

Porteous, A., *The Forest in Folklore and Mythology* (Mineola, 2001)

Rackham, Oliver, *The History of the Countryside: The Full Fascinating Story of Britain's Landscape* (London, 1986)

Russell, Tony, and Catherine Cutler, *The World Encyclopaedia of Trees* (London, 2003)

Taplin, Kim, *Tongues in Trees: Studies in Literature and Ecology* (Totnes, 1989)

Tyler, Michael, *British Oaks: A Concise Guide* (Marlborough, 2008)

Vescoli, Michael, *The Celtic Tree Calendar: Your Tree Sign and You* (London, 1999)

Whitlock, R., *The Oak* (London, 1985)

Associations and Websites

There are many organizations, local national and international concerned with the past, present and future of the oak. Some are primarily concerned with the preservation of ancient trees, which they see as part of our heritage. This involves surveys and reporting threats or the presence of disease. Others are focused on restoring ancient woodlands or planting new ones as an environmental contribution to dealing with global warming. Much of the effort is voluntary, albeit through organizations. As so many are local or regional, providing a short list of organizations would not do justice to the many dedicated people involved in so many countries. A long list trying to cover all their various concerns would be impossible, and still suffer from omissions.

In a changing scene the only quick, satisfactory solution is for those interested in particular aspects of the tree to conduct their own internet search by entering appropriate criteria, for example, oldest oaks + U.S. or oak + diseases. That way, sources of information and organizations dedicated to specific objectives can be identified swiftly. Links to other relevant sites soon become evident. It is a good cause.

Acknowledgements

Encouragingly, the broad subject-matter of this book has stirred the enthusiasm of many people, who have come forward with information and useful suggestions. Principal among them are Barbara Abbs, Kath Baldwin, Luke Barley, Jean Bates, Marion Boughton, Ikram Chaudhry, Peter Crosskey, Gillian Dewdney, Carol Dyhouse, David Elliott, Chris Firth, Monica Guy, Denise Holt, Anita Hooper, Anna Johnston, Lawrence Long, Peter Martin, Helena Martinova, Douglas Matthews, Professor Hugh Pritchard, Terry Pullin, Paul Reader, Judy and Trevor Stokes, Geoffrey Stevenson, Deryck Weatherall, Ed Welfare, Simon Young.

Among the institutions that have been helpful are British Waterways; Centerparcs; Central Council of Church Bell Ringers; Chiswick House and Gardens Trust; City Commons, City of London Corporation; Crawley Public Library; Downlands Trust; Forestry Commission; Fortune's of Whitby; Gonville and Caius College, Cambridge; Jack Daniel's; Kent Woodturners; Jim Beam; John Jameson & Son Ltd; McCurdy & Co. Ltd; Millennium Seed Bank; The National Trust; Normandy Tourist Office; Nottinghamshire County Council; Scotch Whisky Association; Sheffield Galleries and Museums; Sussex Woodcraft Society; West Sussex Library Service; Wooden Canal Boat Society; Woodland Trust.

Photo Acknowledgements

The author and publishers wish to express their thanks to the below sources of illustrative material and/or permission to reproduce it.

From R. Ackermann, *The Microcosm of London: or London in Miniature*, vol. III (London, 1904): p. 47; Alte Nationalgalerie, Berlin: p. 165; photo Anguskirk: pp. 8–9; photo Phil Armitage: p. 35; photos Jean Bates: pp. 127, 133, 180–81; photo Stefano Bolognini: p. 105; photos © Trustees of the British Museum, London: pp. 25, 145, 146; photo Graham Calow (www.naturespot.org.uk): p. 185; photo www.cepolina.com: p. 12; photo George Chernilevsky: p. 38; © 2012 Michael Craig-Martin: pp. 158–9; photo Daderot: pp. 66–7; photo Danish Mediaeval Centre, Nykøbing, Denmark: p. 91; Feodosiya Art Gallery, Crimea: p. 74; photo courtesy Ferriby Heritage Trust, Beverley: p. 64; photo Paul Ferris: p. 149; Collection of the Guild of St George, Museums Sheffield: p. 164; photo Ji-Elle: p. 42; courtesy the Estate of Anna Johnston: p. 15; Kensington Palace, London: p. 117; photo © Graham Kenward 2012: p. 33; photo Kings Lynn Museum: p. 40; photo kukka jpn: p. 18; photo Michael Leaman / Reaktion Books: pp. 16–17; Lenbachhaus Museum, Munich: p. 171 (foot); Metropolitan Museum of Art, New York: p. 167 (foot); Murauchi Art Museum, Tokyo: p. 167 (top); Museum of Fine Arts, Houston, Texas: p. 171 (top); Museum of Russian Art, Kiev: p. 154; reproduced courtesy of the artist (David Nash) and Yorkshire Sculpture Park, Wakefield (www.ysp.co.uk): 160; Collection of the National Gallery of Australia, Canberra: pp. 158–9; photo National Trust / Gillian Dewdney: p. 53; Nationalmuseet, Copenhagen: p. 105; Norwich Castle Museum and Art Gallery (photo © Norfolk Museums and Archaeology Service): p. 29 (foot); photo Poznań Musuem / Robert Wrzesiński: p. 31; private collections: pp. 134, 153, 156, 157, 160; photo Chris Pye woodcarver: p. 116; Rijksmuseum, Amsterdam: p. 151; photo Wenche Samnøy: p. 68; photo Barry Slemmings: p. 41; courtesy stephentaylorpaintings.com: 156, 157; from Johann Georg Sturm, *Deutschlands Flora in Abbildungen* (Nürnberg, 1862): p. 6; Szepmuveszeti Museum, Budapest: p. 152; photo W. L. Tarbert: p. 29 (top); photo Tortipede: p. 150; Victoria and Albert Museum, London: p. 55; photo Viva-Verdi: p. 71; Vikingskipshuset, Oslo, Norway: pp. 66–7; Wadsworth Athenaeum, Hartford, Connecticut: p. 174; photo Michael Wal: p. 85; photo wavering: p. 88; photo Wikimedia / Jarosław Pocztarski: p. 186

Index